PLACES OF WORSHIP

Introduction by James S. Russell

The places of Christian worship in this anthology show the very diverse ways in which spiritual needs and aspirations can be expressed in architectural form. None of these churches fits gracefully into the easy pluralism of our age, rather each represents a distinct, singular worldview.

Perhaps only the two churches of Tadao Ando could be thought of as 'ecumenical' in character, reflecting the non-doctrinaire nature of Christianity in Japan. Yet the stark image of the cross in Ando's work is somehow the most naked image of spirituality present in any of these projects. One cross rises out of the water; another is lit from behind by a mysterious light; four of them forebodingly enclose a transitional space of ambiguous purpose. This stripped-clean, uninflected cruciform presence is out of character with the emotional coolness so typical of the architect's work.

By contrast, Sir Christopher Wren's St Paul's Cathedral, intended to give architectural expression to the humanistic aims of the reformed Church of England, appears to present-day eyes – and I dare say would have appeared to the eyes of its contemporaries – as emotionally neutral, almost institutional in character. The building does not call overtly upon a higher power as the Gothic style it so willfully avoided would. Instead, the cathedral is, for all intents these days, a civic monument, its dome – rising out of the cityscape majestically – still the emblematic image of the City of London.

The most moving of the three projects may well be Jože Plečnik's Church of the Sacred Heart in Prague, if for no other reason than that its emotional content is so rawly expressed, so questing and unfinished.

Wren's design process is perhaps the strangest for contemporary eyes to comprehend, in that the architect came to his design in a monotheistic age, choosing to deploy pragmatic, secular means of architectural expression. Wren thought that spirituality would emerge from finding the most perfect 'natural' form for architecture. St Paul's is, as Vaughan Hart's text tells us, the 'product of a mathematically defined universe,' conceived and refined through the recently popularized use of perspective projection, and therefore ordered by optical means. Wren felt that the orders of architecture reflected a connection with nature – columns and porticos representing the trunks and branches of the forest. Today, when nature is largely the province of science, Wren's vision seems more secular still.

Wren's masterpiece, however, has never been critically eclipsed as so many other great works have. Wren may have found constructional necessity an aesthetic inconvenience – burying the gothic buttresses and brick oval dome in a Portland-stone carapace more pleasing to the eye – but the very clarity of his focus on aesthetic means and ends has produced a work of ineffable rightness. Critics have picked it apart: what was he thinking of when he surmounted two sets of paired columns on the west front? Should he not have adopted a more fluid, Baroque rendering of the Latin cross plan? However, the genius of the building is subtle and distinct, especially when compared (as it so often is) to its nominal model, St Peter's in Rome. (Hart's essay shows the two together.) St Peter's, the product of twelve architects to St Paul's one, is actually a more unified composition. In articulating a design of more distinct parts, however, Wren creates a more inviting and less bombastic building, in keeping with the more congregation-centred nature of the English church's ceremony. Moreover, in comparison to St Peter's, Wren's great dome is narrower, lighter and loftier, which is surprising considering the visual weight with which it presides over the London skyline.

The paradigmatic world occupied by Wren saw nature as, at best, an entity to be put to use; at worst, something fearsome and even evil, requiring the taming hand of man. Tadao Ando, in contrast, evokes nature in a much more literal way, presenting its actuality as part of the architecture of the Church on the Water. This approach, which reflects the Japanese understanding of nature as benign or even admirable, has not been lost among those who have converted to Christianity. At the Church on the Water, Ando is able to focus the project on a vista of idealized (yet hardly wild) nature. Indeed, Ando uses architecture to unleash the spiritual power of light, water and the natural landscape. The path into the chapel proper is so elaborate and so marked by architectural events that the experience of entering it is akin to an initiation ceremony. What the entrance sequence achieves is a preparation for the elaborately framed vista of water, cross, trees and distant hills which greets the visitor. Ando thereby succeeds in making extraordinary – worthy of contemplation if not outright worship – what would, in other circumstances, be an attractive but ordinary view.

While Wren's church celebrates its position in the city and architecturally partakes of the city's life, Ando's work invariably shuts out the cacophony of the Japanese urban environment, wrapping transcendently calm space, accessed only by elaborate itineraries in high walls with few penetrations. This is true of the Church of the Light, in spite of its modesty of size and simplicity of programme. Nature appears primarily in the form of light blazing through a cruciform slot situated behind the place of the celebrant. The crucifix afire, especially when drawn the height and width of the worship room, is a fearsome sight. One might say it is intended to evoke zealotry; if it were not for the fact that in this Osaka church, as in the Church on the Water, the power of the iconic image is made ambiguous by its detailing as an architectonic element.

This crucifix is also a light slot that divides the elevation into four neat quadrants, a very architectural device, typical of Ando's proportioning system. At the Church on the Water, only the cross in the pond is purely a religious symbol. The concrete crosses in the upper-level, open-air anteroom could be grave markers or they could be simply architectonic emblems, echoing the criss-cross of the window mullions behind them to which they are aligned. Or is it the other way round: do the mullions' pattern take on religious character by echoing that of the crosses?

Plečnik's project is instantly recognizable as Christian through its use of the conventional elements of church architecture – nave and tower – however simplified in massing and however unique in imagery is the Prague church. Just as Wren carefully considered the open, urban location of St Paul's and the streets that its chief portals would face, so Plečnik orchestrated his building's mass to punctuate the view from several vantage points along streets that spill into the Jiříz Poděbrad Square. Yet the Plečnik church's way of projecting its power is entirely different to that of either Wren's or Ando's buildings. Plečnik, who donated his services to this project as it became increasingly protracted, chose motifs to invest the final project with the religious fervour he himself felt. It is evocative, expressionistic, even mannered – in short, everything that Ando's and Wren's buildings are not.

In spite of the 'classical' symmetry of the Church of the Sacred Heart taken as a whole, there is a Victorian quality to the textile-like treatment of the exterior; the wide palette of colour and texture that is also reminiscent of the emotion-driven work of the nineteenth-century American architect, Frank Furness, of Philadelphia. Furness was extremely free in his use of Gothic and exotic motifs (critics argued he simply did not know when to quit). He deployed these devices to create a visually riveting proto-industrial tectonic: columns become plunging pistons; massive, encrusted cornices appear to crush the body of the building on its massive, battered foundations. The Church of the Sacred Heart has a similar sense of alternating compression and expansion, of motion and incompletion. The alternation of render and brick in the base makes the building look as if some seismic event crushed the nave against the sacristy, explosively extruding the slab of the tower as a slice of ecclesiastically flavoured toast. The tower, moreover, is the most 'Furnessian' element of the building. Its brooding heaviness is made ambiguous by the huge transparent clock. Why, one might ask, did Plečnik design a clock for the tower? It completely overwhelms the cross at the top, which should be the most important element of the tower. Similarly, the tower of Furness' Fine Arts Library at the University of Pennsylvania is opened up by an enormous yet entirely functionless Gothic window. (Furthermore, Plečnik installed a wonderfully fluid International-Style ramp in his tower, accessible, presumably only by maintenance personnel. Furness included an ornately detailed stair in his Library, which attenuates drastically as it rises, twirling indecisively within the vast space of the tower, because the upper reaches of this extravaganza actually serve only a few subsidiary spaces.)

It is, however, the very strangeness of Plečnik's composition that gives such evocative power to what is actually a rather modest building erected on a tight budget. Each element of the design is individually intriguing, and seems a discovery – the output of a prodigious imagination. Though not a picturesque composition, the

church's deployment of motifs is episodic. It comes together, but does so according to Plečnik's rules, which gives the design a tenuous quality. The building involves the visitor in answering the riddles it presents. Do the obelisks, for example, belong to the 'Roman' tower or do they act as the culmination of the side-entrance slot of the 'neo-Grec' mass of the building? Should the garlands more literally 'hang' from something? Why are there wedge-like projections over the doors?

The interior raises more questions. For all its modernist horizontality and Functionalist references, the brass studs embedded in the walls and the bronze statuary and monumental marble altar assemblage evoke oriental and Egyptian precedents. Ivan Margolius' text says this work's 'singular and startling' conception forces the visitor to 'reflect actively on and interact with Plečnik's creation'. It is in this way that the architect hoped to allow the worshipper to separate himself from the outside world and fully partake in the ritual of the church service. Given the meagre means at his disposal, compared to the sprawling Church on the Water and the spectacle of St Paul's, it becomes a powerful statement.

Such diverse approaches to church building are followed through in the treatment of the very fabric of each of these buildings. For all their visual diversity there is again, an odd commonality between Wren's and Ando's approach. Hybridizing a Gothic nave, a Roman dome and a Byzantine dome-support-system seemed perfectly reasonable to Wren if it helped him realize his aesthetic goals. Thus, even though the columns, entablatures and domes iconographically 'describe' the way the building is built (recall the references to tree trunks and branches), much of what we see in St Paul's is not architectural truth. The top level of the two-storey pilaster and entablature system used on the north and south elevations is simply a monumental parapet screening the Gothic buttressing system. The resulting narrow nave allows glorious amounts of light to spill in, however, making this a far less gloomy place than later churches with wider naves and higher side aisles. Likewise, Wren disguises the elongated brick dome that actually holds up the exterior and interior visible shells.

Ando is 'honest' about his materials. The concrete is both facing and structure. Glass and metal do not pose for what they are not. However, Ando's palette, like Wren's, is a means to an end, not an end in itself as its highly assertive nature would suggest. Not only is Ando's palette of materials almost unvarying from project to project, it is used for the same purpose: to edit the user's experiences so he or she will only appreciate what is desired. At the Church on the Water, the glass-enclosed anteroom opens to the sky. The visitor immediately notices this, and it helps focus appreciation for sky and nature, just as the chapel, in its singular focus on the landscape, asks the viewer to consider that. Sliding back the full-height glazed door further intensifies the experience because the smell of earth and trees and the sound of water are much more intensely experienced where least expected, in an otherwise completely enclosed room.

The angled wall of the Church of the Light operates similarly, allowing bands of light to move across the otherwise undifferentiated interior walls. The worshipper becomes aware not of the walls themselves but of the light and its movement as the day passes, not the walls themselves.

Plečnik's approach to building fabric is less cerebral than that of Wren or Ando. There is no Gothic evocation of heaven nor any modernist technological exhibitionism. The roof, for example is supported by a conventional truss, clad with a traditional coffered ceiling. The enclosure, too, is little modulated. Instead, Plečnik lavished his attention on the juxtaposition of materials and details. The alternation of light and dark, of the prickly brick and stone surface versus the soft-edged, smooth render ask the viewer to engage the fabric of the building. The proportions of the interior offer, by contrast, the transcendent calm of the golden section. Akin to the exterior, though, the heft of the exposed brick walls inside is softened by the band of high windows and the lightness of their plastered surrounds.

The fervour that drives much religious architecture often embodies the belief that there is only one path to righteousness. Plečnik's architecture addresses religious feeling most directly. On its own, the building's intensity and idiosyncrasy are readily digested; pleasant surprises turn up everywhere, as Plečnik's form-making facility appears to be unbounded. Compared to the other projects in this anthology, however, there is a whiff of the fundamentalist, the *Mitteleuropa* mystic. And when it comes to the spiritual, the true believers have a way of undermining the comfortable compartmentalization of religion and daily life that is so much the province of 'reasonable' people in a secular age. Yet the diversity of great religious architecture (of which these buildings represent but a tiny snapshot) could be seen as undermining the single-path-to-salvation sensibility. The entire œuvre of Ando, Wren and Plečnik has a spiritual quality even though the spiritual *zeitgeist* of each is spectacularly different, as is the built result. Ando manipulates light from mysterious sources and interplays light, nature and building fabric. Plečnik more literally explored and invested spirituality in the motifs he chose. Wren thought spirituality would emerge from mathematical and optical correctness.

In these, as well as other important religious buildings, the beliefs of the religion *per se* may only be indirectly or abstractly represented in the architecture. Of course, many spectacular places of worship are little more than armatures for iconography – renderings of a gospel in stone. The projects in this anthology show that architecture is capable of more; that it can inspire a kind of alchemy, preparing the worshipper to receive the spiritual experience. The shepherding – and enclosure – of the experience, which is beyond the province of any one religion or ceremony, remains universal and perpetually available for reconsideration by architects with insight and talent.

Sir Christopher Wren
St Paul's Cathedral
London 1675–1710

Vaughan Hart

Photography
Angelo Hornak; cover detail
also by Angelo Hornak
Drawings
Arthur Poley

1

From Magical Cosmos to Mathematical Universe

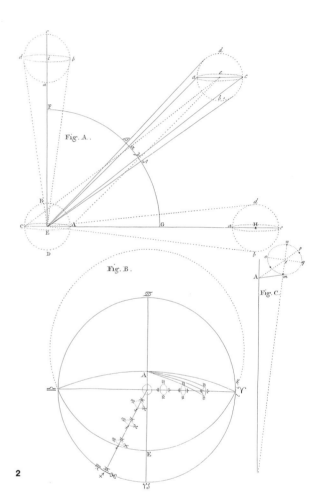

2

Wren's temple to the new nature

Christopher Wren was born in 1632, one year before Inigo
Jones started his ill-fated refacing of St Paul's Cathedral, and
died in 1723 at the grand age of 91 having carried to completion
the centrepiece of his age, a new Cathedral built on the ashes
of the old. St Paul's had taken 35 years to build, few Cathedrals
of comparable grandeur having been constructed by a single
architect within his own lifetime. Indeed, probably no previous
English Cathedral had been designed entirely by one man. Unlike
Jones, Wren never visited Rome to study antiquity, but his brief
visit to Paris to escape the plague in 1665 allowed him to witness
at first hand forms such as the dome, of which England possessed
no examples until Wren's work, and to meet leading continental
Baroque architects including Bernini. It is, however, principally in
the context of the emerging mathematical sciences of the Royal
Society that we should understand Wren's approach to, and
development of, traditional Renaissance theories on architecture
and hence his intentions behind St Paul's. For having become the
Professor of Astronomy at Gresham College at the age of 25,
his early achievements were not in fact in architecture at all but
in the sciences. When Wren turned to architecture five years
later, it represented more a change in employment than in
intellectual outlook.

   Wren's life spanned the period in which the magical,
or Platonic, conception of nature, expressed in the works
of Shakespeare and Jones,[1] was replaced by that of a
mathematically defined universe determined by experiment.[2]
This shift had an inevitable impact throughout the arts in their
representation of nature. Following Newton's discovery of the
equality of the force of action and reaction, the use of
symmetry in particular came to reflect natural laws rather
than the Platonic conception of the figure of man as
a microcosm, whilst through their use of linear perspective,
architects harnessed the idea of spatial infinity which was central
to the emerging conception of the universe. However, this new
philosophy emerged from and absorbed many features of the
established order; despite his part in the formulation of the new
sciences, Wren himself evidently maintained a faith in aspects of
medieval magical lore.[3] In 1660, the year of Charles II's restoration,
Wren played a critical role in the institutionalization of the early
sciences represented by the founding of the Royal Society which,
in following the principles of Francis Bacon, was dedicated
to enquiry into natural phenomena through observation and
not received tradition.[4] This included the study of the
mathematical science of architecture, its building materials
and structural systems exemplified by Wren's roof truss used
in the Sheldonian Theatre, Oxford (1664–9), which had been
presented to the Society in 1663.

   Wren's first application of the mathematical sciences
to architecture dates from 1661 and his move from London
to Oxford as Savilian Professor of Astronomy. Wren was to
continue his investigations into the sciences throughout his life,
serving as the Royal Society's President between 1681–3,
although architecture became the principal expression of this
interest. His first architectural commissions – the supervision of
the construction of the fortification at Tangier (which he declined)
and the repair of Old St Paul's Cathedral – were a result of his
acknowledged ability at geometry and mechanics in their relation

to architecture, rather than any proven mastery of the rules of 'antique' design derived from the Roman author Vitruvius. Wren's study was limited to the Renaissance treatises read alongside the architecture of Jones, together with Fréart de Chambray's *Parallèle de l'Architecture antique et de la moderne* (1650), the adaptation of the Vitruvian rules in Claude Perrault's *Ordonnance des cinq espèces de colonnes selon la méthode des Anciens* (1683)[5] and by the Baroque architecture of Paris. Wren's education illustrates the shift in priority from a knowledge of the treatise and the monuments of Rome to that of mathematics and geometry as the guarantor of architectural good practice. Indeed Wren lamented that 'It seems very unaccountable, that the Generality of our late Architects dwell so much upon this ornamental, and so slightly pass over the geometrical, which is the most essential Part of Architecture.'[6]

This observation is to be found in the second of five 'Tracts' in which Wren outlined his theory of architecture. These were written from around 1675 but were published posthumously by his grandson in *Parentalia: Or, Memoirs of the Family of the Wrens* (1750). In shifting attention from the study of astronomical and geometric theory to architectural practice, Wren sought to define architectural laws in the spirit of the new 'experimental' philosophy. Indeed Wren's theories redefining architectural history and beauty can be seen as fundamental to the structure, form and style of his Cathedral. For having written the Tracts, so far as is known, during the period in which he worked on the Cathedral, the recommendations so clearly defined within them cannot have been ignored by their author in the realization of his great temple.

Architectural history and St Paul's Cathedral

Wren's attempt to return to first principles in his study of nature also prompted his re-evaluation of the antique mythology which had underpinned Renaissance architecture. Recent discoveries seemed to prove the fallibility of the ancients, and the moderns were therefore obliged to reassess the role of antiquity as the source for architectural principles. In this spirit Wren himself noted 'how much the Mathematical Wits of this Age have excell'd the Ancients, (who pierc'd but to the Bark and Outside of Things) in handling particular Disquisitions of Nature'; he adds that a vital part of this process lay 'in clearing up History, and fixing Chronology',[7] thus foreshadowing Newton's *Chronology of the Ancient Kingdoms Amended* (1728). Through travel books describing the New World and the Near and Far East[8] and, closer to home, investigations into enigmatic monuments such as Stonehenge, the Royal Society became increasingly aware of buildings with antique attributes which seemed outside the accepted historical development of architecture. In his 'Tracts on Architecture', therefore, Wren outlined his view of the origin and early history of architecture in an attempt to 'reform the Generality to a truer taste in Architecture by giving a larger Idea of the whole Art, beginning with the reasons and progress of it from the most remote Antiquity',[9] and in so doing discovered the universal 'Principles' or 'Grounds of Architecture'[10] central to his work at St Paul's.

Despite this rational intent, but compatible with his acceptance of aspects of magical cosmology, Wren's historical scheme was still in fact dependent on the two most important sources for architectural history formulated in the Renaissance – the Bible and Vitruvius. Vitruvius' *De Architectura* owed its enduring status to the fact that it was the only surviving record of antique building practices, whilst as

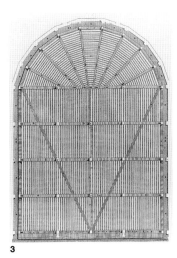

3

1 Portrait of Wren and his Cathedral by Johann Baptist Closterman, 1683.
2 Wren's study of planetary motion from *Parentalia*, London, 1750.
3 Wren's roof truss for the Sheldonian Theatre, Oxford, from *Parentalia*.

4 The primitive hut according to Cesariano's *Vitruvius*, Como, 1521.
5 Wren prefigured the presentation of the primitive hut as the origin of the Orders by Marc-Antoine Laugier in his *Essai sur l'Architecture*, Paris, 1753.

EX PRIMA MVNDI HOMINVM AETATE AEDIFICATIO. MVLTI ENIM AB ANIMALIBVS EXEMPLA VITAE CONSERVAE QꝪ IMITATI SVNT &ca

4

5

6

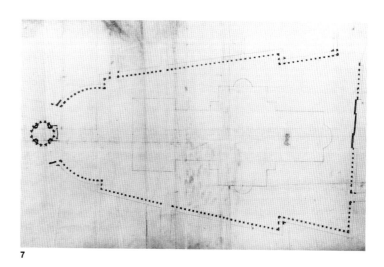

7

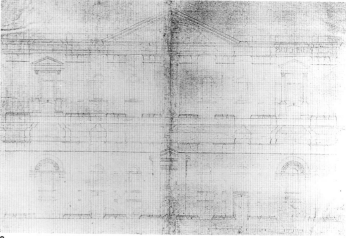

8

a Christian Wren accepted the notion that, alongside Nature, Scripture revealed divine laws. In amending both sources to make one coherent history, Wren rejected those Renaissance architectural theories which for the most part had reflected the old cosmology. Most significantly, in Tract I Wren identified the origin of the Orders with the description by Vitruvius of primitive man's construction of huts from branches (II, i, 2–7),[11] and in so doing rejected the Roman author's subsequent more explicit analogy of the Orders to human proportions (IV, i, 6–8). According to Wren, 'in the hot Countries, where Civility first began, they desired to exclude the Sun only, and admit all possible Air for Coolness and Health: this brought in naturally the Use of Porticoes, or Roofs for Shade, set upon Pillars'; in this 'we see they imitated Nature, most Trees in their Prime … This I think the more natural Comparison, than that to the Body of a Man, in which there is little Resemblance of a cylindrical Body'.[12] The column here followed natural laws for practical as opposed to symbolic reasons, prefiguring the arguments in Marc-Antoine Laugier's famous *Essai sur l'Architecture* published over a half century later, in 1753. A sign of this rationalization is that the Orders themselves preoccupy Wren much less than they had Renaissance commentators on architecture. Directly echoing Perrault's *Ordonnance*,[13] Wren goes on to reject the idea of 'perfect' Pythagorean proportions for the Orders as formulated by Serlio and his successors, noting at the outset of Tract II that proportions were 'more arbitrarily used than they care to acknowledge', and that these have been reduced 'into Rules, too strict and pedantick, and so as not to be transgressed, without the Crime of Barbarity'.[14] Indeed, at St Paul's the pairing of the Orders and the two-tier portico on the west front dramatically depart from established rules.

The novel two-tier portico had been forced on Wren by the lack of stone blocks long enough to span a giant portico on the scale aspired to in the 'Great Model'.[15] Despite the lack of an obvious antique precedent for such a portico, porticoes themselves were thought by Wren to replicate a natural prototype. For in Tract II he noted that trees had provided shade around the first cellas, and that 'when the Temples were brought into Cities, the like Walks were represented with Stone Pillars'. The arcade surrounding St Paul's as drawn by Nicholas Hawksmoor (1661/2–1736), Wren's assistant from about 1680, can be seen as an attempt to realize this primitive original, albeit on a grand scale. For Wren himself adds that such arcades were 'the true Original of Colonades environing the Temples in single or double Ailes'.[16] These trees were also the origin of porticoes, for according to Wren, 'these Avenues were afterwards, as Cities grew more wealthy, reformed into Porticoes of Marble', although, as the portico at St Paul's suggests, these trees were 'not equally growing' in their spacing. The proportions of the Orders were even formed in imitation of trees, for 'at first the Columns were six Diameters in Heighth; when the Imitation of Groves was forgot, the Diameters were advanced to seven; then to eight; then to nine, as in the *Ionick* Order; then, at last, to ten, as in the *Corinthian* and *Italick* Orders'. He adds that 'slender Columns would leave them more Opportunity to shew their Skill in carving and enriching their Works in the Capitals and Mouldings'.[17] As a temple intended to proclaim this ultimate refinement of the Orders, Wren put these ideas into practice at St Paul's, for the lower, forty-foot high Corinthian Order is indeed proportioned using ten modules[18] as examples of the design drawings illustrate. The upper Italic, or Composite, Order is however slightly taller in proportion; this may have been to accommodate

9

optical distortions, following Wren's theory of natural beauty, with its dependence on optical effect, which will be examined shortly.

Wren called the first primitive timber column the 'Tyrian', or Phoenician Order, following its supposed use by masons from Tyre, a city in Phoenicia, in the building of the Temple of Solomon. Wren adds that 'from these *Phoenicians* I derive, as well the Arts, as the Letters of the *Grecians*, though it may be the *Tyrians* were Imitators of the *Babylonians*, and they of the *Egyptians*'.[19] In embracing pre-classical antiquity, this progression in refinement from Tyrian timber column to the Orders of Greek antiquity seemed to account for such primitive stone monuments as Stonehenge. As a consequence, in the spirit of Baroque ornamentation, Wren undermined the Renaissance canon of five Orders; there had been many legitimate types of Orders, for 'The Orders are not only *Roman* and *Greek*, but *Phoenician*, *Hebrew*, and *Assyrian*' and as such were 'founded upon the Experience of all Ages'.[20] Based on his study of Gothic Cathedrals, Wren even recognized the 'Saracen style' invented by the Arabs and imported by the returning Crusaders as a valid legacy from which to learn. However, in Wren's own work, the Gothic was largely consumed within forms derived from antiquity, reflecting his criteria for natural beauty. Wren's entrance gate at Christ Church College in Oxford (1681–2), Tom Tower, is only superficially a 'Gothic' tower with its strict symmetry and dome, whilst the design of St Paul's utilized – albeit by necessity – and concealed Gothic structural techniques and forms.

Wren thus established the authority and continued validity of the Orders which he displayed on St Paul's through their use on the archetypal temple, although having developed from the primitive hut the Orders themselves were now derived from a man-made structure and not from a divine pattern as Renaissance tradition held. Wren necessarily dismissed as 'a fine romantick Piece' and 'mere Fancy'[21] the Solomonic Corinthian Order first published in 1604 by Juan Bautista Villalpando. Villalpando's illustrations, with their reflection of Pythagorean mysticism, still had influence in England, however. One of the commissioners for the repair of the Old Cathedral, John Evelyn, in translating Fréart's *Parallèle* in 1664 illustrated the 'Corinthian Profile *of the* Temple of Solomon *out of* Villalpandus',[22] whilst, in dedicating to Wren *An Account of Architects and Architecture* (1706), Evelyn reported on the translation that 'going to St *Paul's*, to Contemplate that *August Pile,* and the Progress You have made, some of Your *Chief Work-men*, gratefully Acknowledging the Assistance it had afforded them'. Evelyn's Solomonic Order would have been of especial use to these masons, naturally more traditional in outlook, in their carving of the Corinthian portico at St Paul's.

In the Tracts Wren proposed a logical form, plan and structure for ancient buildings constructed during Old Testament times. From Genesis he took the first city of Enos, proceeding in Tract V to Noah's Ark, the Tower of Babel and the pyramids of Egypt. He included examples of Tyrian monuments: the Temple of Dagon destroyed by Samson is reconstructed against structural principles in Tract IV, and the sepulchre of Absalom and Temple of Solomon are described in Tract V. Wren also studied buildings dating from early antiquity: the Tyrian sepulchre of the Etruscan King Porsenna is outlined at the end of Tract V, whilst the Temple of Diana at Ephesus, as the first building to employ the Ionic Order, and the sepulchre of Mausolus built with the Doric at Halicarnassus are discussed at the end of Tract IV. Here Wren also studied the Temple of Peace (Basilica of Maxentius) and the Augustan Temple of Mars Ultor which he followed Pliny in placing

6 Wren's 'Great Model' of the Greek cross scheme for St Paul's, 1673.
7 Nicholas Hawksmoor's drawing for an arcade surrounding the Cathedral.
8 Wren's design drawing for the portico showing ten modules for the lower Order.
9 'Tom Tower', entrance gate at Christ Church College, Oxford, 1681–2.
10 Solomon's temple according to J B Villalpando, from *In Ezechielem Explanationes et Apparatus Urbis ac Templi Hierosolymitani*, III vols, Rome, 1596–1604.
11 Pillar of Absalom from Le Brun's *Voyage au Levant*, Paris, 1714.
12 Sepulchre of Porsenna from John Greaves' *Pyramidographia: or a description of the pyramids in Egypt*, London, 1646.

11

10

12

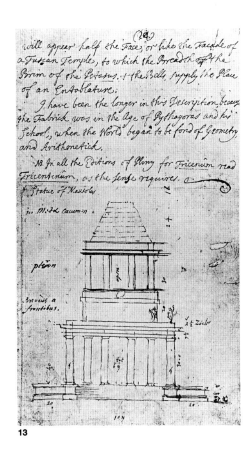

13

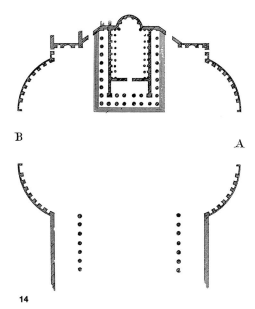

B   A

14

15

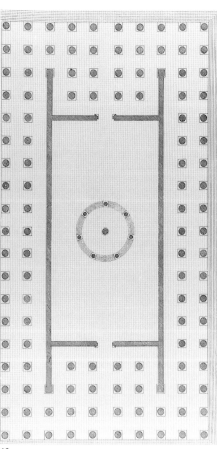

16

alongside the Pantheon as 'the most remarkable Works of *Rome*'.[23] The Temple of Peace had been incorporated into biblical history by Renaissance commentators as the supposed repository for 'the Spoils of the *Jewish* Temple, and the Records of *Rome*, the most sacred for Antiquity' as Wren himself observed.[24]

Wren's concentration on the physical properties of the archetypes of architectural mythology and his analysis of the technical requirements of their construction found a contemporary echo in the work of the German philosopher Anastasis Kircher, whose attempt to quantify Noah's Ark and the Tower of Babel appeared as *Arca Noe* in Amsterdam in 1675.[25] In Wren's hands legends cultivated by the medieval masonry guilds become proof that architecture was a branch not of arcane knowledge but of his own mathematical sciences; thus Wren commented in Tract V that 'the Sons of Seth, the other son of Adam, erected two Columns of Brick and Stone to preserve their Mathematical Sciences to Posterity'.[26] This echoed the general decline of Renaissance architecture, with its proportional systems reflecting the Platonic harmony of a finite cosmos of concentrically orbiting planets, and its eclipse by the freer Baroque style of oval forms and broken pediments, clearly demonstrating the breakdown of the Vitruvian canon and the formulation of an open, infinite universe of elliptical planetary motion.[27] In fact Wren's architecture is neither Renaissance nor Baroque on the continental model, and is perfectly compatible with his rationalization of the more practical aspects of Renaissance Vitruvian and biblical mythology within the context of the mathematical sciences, themselves still based on certain Renaissance magical theories. Hence what we see in Wren's 'style' at St Paul's is not a compromise, as commentators have tended

to claim,[28] but a unique synthesis of the Renaissance and Baroque which represented his coherent view of history and nature.

From his re-evaluation of history Wren aimed to identify principles of architecture with an eternal validity akin to those of the mathematical sciences. In this spirit St Paul's was intended to celebrate the conclusion of the historical development of the Orders themselves, from the primitive hut through Solomon's 'Tyrian' Order to the great Corinthian temple in London. The Cathedral should be seen as Wren's attempt to proclaim the timelessness of his architectural principles carved in stone, for following his French visit he had reacted against the excess of Baroque ornamentation in noting that 'Works of Filgrand, and little Knacks are in great Vogue; but Building certainly ought to have the Attribute of eternal',[29] whilst later, in Tract I, he elaborates that 'Architecture aims at Eternity; and therefore the only Thing uncapable of Modes and Fashions in its Principals, [are] the *Orders*'.[30]

Historical models and the design of St Paul's Cathedral

Wren's Tracts represent a rewriting of the Renaissance view of history to 'justify' from apparently first principles the use of historical models in his own work. For Wren based his Cathedral design on specific models studied in the Tracts. His use of porticoes to screen the building fabric at Greenwich Hospital and St Paul's clearly reflected his view of the development of the antique city outlined in Tract III, for example, since in building Alexandria Dinocrates 'drew a long Street with Porticoes on both Sides', after which 'they soon filled the Quarters between the Porticoes with private and publick Buildings. Thus were Cities suddenly raised'.[31] Following his reappraisal of architectural development to include newly discovered monuments and styles, Wren commended structural techniques drawn from Byzantine architecture in advising: 'you may build upon that Circle an upright Wall, which may bear a Cupola again above, as is done at *St Sophia*'; he adds that 'I question not but those at *Constantinople* had it from the *Greeks* before them, it is so natural'. In comparing the Gothic arch with this 'eastern Way of Vaulting by Hemispheres', Wren makes clear his use of the latter system 'in the vaulting of the Church of *St Paul's*'.[32] This demonstrates the growing awareness of Byzantine architecture in England, for Wren had never visited Constantinople but based his observations on the description by the traveller John Greaves.[33] He possibly discussed St Sophia with Fischer Von Erlach during the German architect's visit to London in 1704, for Von Erlach's *Entwurff einer Historische Architectur* begun a year later includes St Sophia as part of a pictorial presentation embracing Eastern and Chinese monuments in a 'historicist' re-reading of architectural development along the lines of Wren's Tracts.

As the standard Renaissance source for the rotunda and centralized church, the Pantheon formed Wren's obvious model in his design of the Cathedral's domed central space. Indeed Wren's son noted that in forming a 'great Cupola' of 112 feet in diameter, 'the *Surveyor* has imitated the *Pantheon*, or *Rotundo* in *Rome*, excepting only that the upper Order is there but umbratile, not extant as at St *Paul's*, out of the Wall'. He adds that the '*Pantheon* is no higher within than its Diameter; St *Peter's* is two Diameters; this seems too high, the other too low; the *Surveyor* at St *Paul's* took a mean Proportion'.[34] This reflection of the Pantheon is obviously emphasized by the painted coffering and oculus lighting the dome. Even though Wren thus followed Renaissance practice in basing his designs on antique models, their proportions were clearly adapted due to the new optical principles.

In *Parentalia* Wren's son commended the Temple of Peace as 'certainly the best and most authentic Pattern of a cathedral Church, which must have three Ailes, according to Custom, and be vaulted'.[35] On the basis of illustrations by both Serlio (III fol 59r) and Palladio (IV ch vi), Wren himself praised the 'Greatness of this Temple, the most magificent of old *Rome*', adding that 'it is longer than our *Westminster-hall*, and the middle Nave only, besides the Ailes, is more than a seventh Part broader; in Heighth it exceeds the highest Cathedral now in the World'.[36] These physical characteristics were clearly of greater importance to Wren than any supposed links with Solomon's temple or the glories of Rome, for this temple was an important source in his development of a three-aisle plan, of particular use to a Cathedral intended as an auditory.[37] Having relocated the medieval outdoor pulpit known as 'Paul's Cross' inside the new Cathedral, this emphasis on preaching was a vital aspect of the Protestant service for which St Paul's was planned, although Wren's design for a moveable pulpit reflects its lack of integration in the plan itself. Indeed in Wren's advice drafted in 1708 to the commission considering the general design of Protestant churches he noted: 'in our reformed Religion, it should seem vain to make a *Parish-church larger*, than that all who are present can both hear and see'; whilst for Catholics, 'it is enough if they hear the Murmur of the Mass, and see the Elevation of the Host', English churches 'are to be fitted for Auditories'.[38] In Tract IV Wren identified the Temple of Peace as the origin of the Roman basilica itself,[39] and noted the structural integrity of its form in ascending 'to its vast Heighth each Way, by three Degrees; the mighty Nave is butted by the Ailes, and the Ailes

17

18

19

13 Wren's sketch reconstruction of the Sepulchre of Mausolus, Halicarnassus.
14 Wren's reconstruction of the Augustan temple of Mars Ultor from *Parentalia*.
15, 16 Wren's reconstruction of the temple of Diana at Ephesus from *Parentalia*.

17 Porticoes by Wren at Greenwich Hospital, 1696–1702.
18, 19 Noah's Ark and the Tower of Babel after Kircher from *Arca Noe*, Amsterdam, 1675.

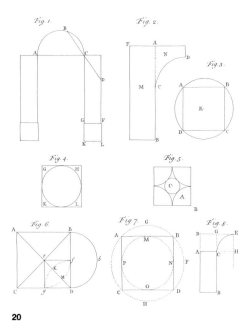

20

21

20 Wren's geometric studies of vaults in Tract II from *Parentalia*.

21 St Sophia, Constantinople, from Fischer Von Erlach's *Entwurff einer Historische Architectur*, Vienna, 1721.

22 Temple of Peace according to Serlio (III, fol 59v).

23 General view of the west front, with its unique two-storey portico of paired columns.

24 North transept portico.

25 South transept portico from the west.

26 Transverse and longitudinal sections through the west portico, drawn by Arthur Poley, published in *St Paul's Cathedral, London, Measured, Drawn and Described*, London, 1927.

by the Tribunals, and little Rooms without … I have admired the Greatness and Firmness of this Pile.'[40] The temple thus provided an antique source for the traditional Cathedral section which had been imposed on Wren at St Paul's by the clergy, whilst enabling him to overcome the inherent problem of lateral thrust generated by aisle vaults which he had observed in Gothic structures such as Salisbury Cathedral.[41] Such neatness of structure was a guiding principle of Wren's mathematics, and his early intention at St Paul's itself was for 'some neate fabrick, wch shall recompence in Art and beauty what it wants in bulke'.[42]

The Temple of Peace clearly informed Wren's design of the internal ornamentation of the Cathedral. For following objections that the main architrave was cut by the great arches, Wren's son reported that 'In this the *Surveyor* always insisted that he had the Ancients on his Side; in the *Templum Pacis*, and in all the great Halls of the Baths, and in all the great Structures of three Ailes, this was done' because 'in those wide Inter-columns the Architrave is not supposed to lye from one great Column to another', and hence 'the End of it will only appear upon the Pillar'.[43] According to Wren, this temple had been used as a hall of justice and was emblematic for the legendary antique Golden Age of peace, since 'No Language, no Poetry can so describe Peace, and the Effects of it in Men's Minds, as the Design of this Temple naturally paints it'.[44] For Wren and his fellow members of the Royal Society their age marked the dawning of a new era of justice and peace; and with St Paul's itself a temple of peace through its clear basis in this antique source, it was appropriate that the Cathedral choir was consecrated on the 2 December 1697, as part of the thanksgiving service following the Treaty of Ryswick marking the end of hostilities between France and England.

Natural beauty and St Paul's Cathedral

Wren introduced the first of his Tracts by echoing the Vitruvian design triad of strength, utility and grace (*firmitas*, *utilitas*, *venustas*, (I, iii, 2)), but now redefined using the epistemology of seventeenth-century science, since 'Beauty, Firmness, and Convenience, are the Principles; the two first depend upon geometrical Reasons of *Opticks* and *Staticks*; the third only makes the Variety'.[45] As a geometrician, for Wren the natural guarantors of firmness or structural integrity were Euclidean principles. When discussing the structure of the Old Cathedral he emphasized his shift from the established design practices of Renaissance architects to those based on geometry, for 'This also may be safely affirm'd, not only by an Architect, taking his Measures from the Precepts and Examples of the Antients, but by a Geometrician, (this part being liable to Demonstration) that the Roof is, and ever was, too heavy for its Butment.'[46] Whilst for the firmness of structure Wren attempted to establish geometric laws based on statics, without which 'a fine Design will fail',[47] the first criterion of design – that is, beauty – was thought less an intrinsic structural quality of the building than it was an optical effect or appearance of geometric purity which worked on the senses of the observer. Like Perrault, Wren recognized in the first of his Tracts two causes of beauty:

Beauty is a Harmony of Objects, begetting Pleasure by the Eye. There are two Causes of Beauty, natural and customary. Natural is from *Geometry*, consisting in Uniformity (that is Equality) and Proportion. Customary Beauty is begotten by the Use of our Senses to those Objects which are usually pleasing to us for other Causes, as Familiarity or particular Inclination breeds a Love of Things not in themselves lovely.

22

23

Here lies the great Occasion of Errors; here is tried the Architect's judgement: but always the true Test is natural or geometric Beauty.[48]

Hence vital to our understanding of Wren's design criteria at St Paul's is the realization that for him there were two *causes*, and not *types*, of beauty. The first cause, based on geometry, included the property of symmetry (here defined as 'equality'), whilst the second was based on familiarity. For Claude Perrault knowledge of the latter alone 'distinguishes true Architects',[49] but for Wren custom was the 'great Occasion of Errors'. Customary causes were outside influences which disturbed the intellect, leading to the apprehension of beauty in objects which had no intrinsic qualities of geometric beauty. Reason was overruled by familiarity and the imagination worked without rules; certain physical aspects were perceived as beautiful, although they were only 'Modes and Fashions' which formed the 'Taste' of a particular age and led to the variations in style which history recorded.

Wren's principle that only 'that which is good of itself is eternal'[50] obviously informed his reassessment of history, and perfectly accorded with the emerging scientific and archaeological approach based on direct observation and the rejection of the customs and legends cultivated in the Renaissance. Architecture was, after all, a mathematical science, and with its strong clarity of geometric forms the Cathedral should be viewed as an attempt to represent this conception of natural beauty following the ancient examples studied in the Tracts. On the Temple of Mars Ultor, for example, Wren comments that the 'Squares in the Wall of the *Cella* opposite to the Inter-columnations, tell us how extremely the Ancients were addicted to square and geometrical Figures, the only natural

Foundation of Beauty'.[51] From the temple's court Wren concluded that 'certainly no Enclosure looks so gracefully as the Circular: 'tis the Circle that equally bounds the Eye, and is every where uniform to itself … a Semicircle joining to an Oblong, as in the Tribunal at the End of this Temple, is a graceful Composition'.[52] This preference lies behind Wren's eastern apse and semi-circular porticoes on the transept facades at St Paul's. Indeed, in its embodiment of pure forms, the Cathedral design clearly followed Wren's hierarchy of geometric beauty, for:

Geometrical Figures are naturally more beautiful than other irregular; in this all consent as to a Law of Nature. Of geometrical Figures, the Square and the Circle are most beautiful; next, the Parallelogram and the Oval. Strait Lines are more beautiful than curve; next to strait Lines, equal and geometrical Flexures; an Object elevated in the Middle is more beautiful than depressed.[53]

It is against the last stipulation that we should understand the Cathedral's west front with its elevated central portico and pediment; and indeed the central dome itself since Wren adds in Tract I that: 'The Ancients elevated the Middle with a Tympan, and Statue, or a Dome.'[54]

Despite this reformulation of the role of beauty in design, from its metaphysical or Platonic reflection of a higher world towards its apparently more rational basis in geometry and optics, the comprehension of beauty was now to rest for Wren on much more empirical judgements of human perception. Echoing Fréart's *Parallèle* of 1650,[55] this theory relied on man's supposed inherent preference for visually balanced, regular geometric forms. In order

24

25

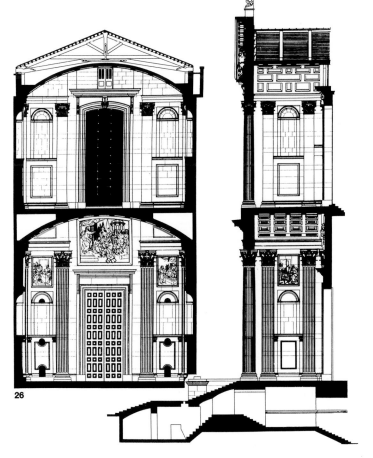

26

27

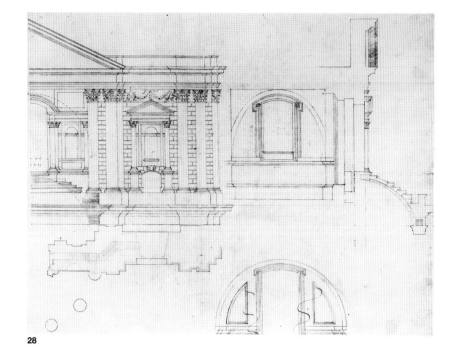

28

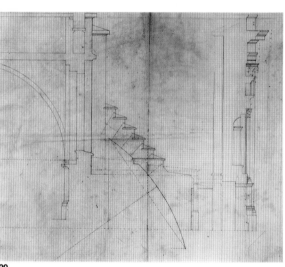

29

to design for this, according to Wren the architect needed to use the optical rules of perspective, taking into account surrounding buildings and viewing distances. The Cathedral was itself evidently designed from drawn perspective views, not judged from models such as those made for the early schemes; for in Tract I Wren specifies that:

The Architect ought, above all Things, to be well skilled in Perspective; for every thing that appears well in the Orthography, may not be good in the Model, especially where there are many Angles and Projectures; and every thing that is good in Model, may not be so when built; because a Model is seen from other Stations and Distances than the Eye sees the Building: but this will hold universally true, that whatsoever is good in Perspective, and will hold so in all the principal Views, whether direct or oblique, will be as good in great, if this only Caution be observed, that Regard be had to the Distance of the Eye in the principal stations.[56]

Accordingly, in elements seen collectively, such as within the simply arranged two-storey ordered block comprising the Cathedral's west front, 'much Variety makes Confusion'. In elements that are seen separately, however, 'great Variety is commendable, provided this Variety transgress not the Rules of *Opticks* and *Geometry*'.[57] An indication that the equally simple side walls of the Cathedral were designed to be viewed in perspective, that is along their length and in total, is found in Wren's comment that the Old Cathedral interior offered 'a pleasing Perspective by the continu'd optical Diminution of the Columns',[58] whilst his son noted that the paired pilasters on the Cathedral sides 'will appear proper to those who consider well the whole Design together'.[59] Indeed in Tract I Wren himself advises that:

In Buildings where the View is sideways, as in Streets … every thing [should be] strait, equal, and uniform. Breaks in the Cornice, Projectures of the upright Members, Variety, Inequality in the Parts, various Heights of the Roof, serve only to confound the Perspective, and make it deformed, while the Breaches and Projectures are cast one upon another, and obscure all Symmetry.[60]

The 'strait, equal, and uniform' might easily describe the Cathedral's side walls, and reads as a triumph of the science of optics and visual simplicity over the distorted forms of Baroque ornamentation. Such optical priorities must equally have governed the overall height of the west front in its relationship to the piazza, and the extent of the clearance of houses which had been a mere 11 feet from the Old Cathedral.[61]

The geometrical clarity of Wren's architecture is frequently divorced from the actual structure or plan of the building, thereby emphasizing this role of geometry as a visual quality over and above its expression of the structural disposition of forces. This is evident in the Cathedral itself, the appearance of which as a two-storey ordered block is achieved by using a screen wall whose principal purpose is to hide the Gothic-style buttresses which support the nave vaults, and thereby also conceal the customary Cathedral form – that is, a high nave with low aisles. This wall fulfils the stabilizing, structural role of Gothic pinnacles which are replaced following Wren's advice in Tract I in which he notes that: 'No sort of Pinnacle is worthy enough to appear in the Air, but Statue. Pyramids are *Gothick*';[62] statues of the apostles are indeed placed against the skyline, with St Paul crowning the portico. Hence this wall was intended as an ordered

30

surface representing natural beauty, replacing and hiding customary (that is, Gothic) practices which were no longer in themselves sources of beauty but provide the subsidiary qualities of firmness in structure and convenience in plan. As such the Cathedral can again be seen to follow Wren's prescriptions in the Tracts, in the second of which he noted that 'the *Romans* never used Buttresses without, but rather within',[63] whilst in the first he advised:

There are only two beautiful Positions of strait Lines, perpendicular and horizontal: this is from Nature, and consequently Necessity, no other than upright being firm. Oblique positions are Discord to the Eye, unless answered in Pairs, as in the Sides of an equicrural Triangle: therefore *Gothick* Buttresses are all ill-favoured, and were avoided by the Ancients, and no Roofs almost but spherick raised to be visible, except in the Front, where the lines answer.[64]

Hence in the Cathedral front the lines of the pediment reflect but conceal the sloping roof, whilst the dome is the only visible roof form. Wren adds that: 'No Roof can have Dignity enough to appear above a Cornice, but the circular.'[65]

Elsewhere in the Cathedral, geometric purity again triumphs over structural functionalism. For whilst the hemispherical dome is created by using three shells, only the inner, brick cone has a structural role, although this, as Wren's son notes, 'he covered and hid out of Sight'.[66] The cone or oval form is more structurally efficient, but possesses less beauty in Wren's hierarchy than the circular. At Cambridge Wren's chapel front at Emmanuel College

(1668–73), with its two symmetrical bays, conceals the true nature of the long, Elizabethan-style gallery behind; at Trinity College library (1676–84) the division of the courtyard facade into two equal arcaded storeys masks the fact that the library's floor is located not at the level of the first-floor entablature but at the lower level of the imposts, making it necessary to fill the lunettes of the arcades which thereby become decorative rather than structural. This is perfectly consistent with Wren's emphasis on visual criteria for beauty but deviates from Gothic and Renaissance traditions – that is, from the clear expression of form and structure in the former and the truthful representation in stone of a timber construction system implicit in the Vitruvian rules of the latter.

For Wren the timeless problem of relating architecture to nature was hence more an exercise in optics than metaphysics; the same optical principles had after all led to the invention of the telescope and microscope for the direct observation of nature itself. On the truth of the new philosophy and its 'Elliptical Astronomy', Wren concluded that: 'For natural Philosophy [has] of late been order'd into a geometrical Way of reasoning from ocular Experiment, that it might prove a real Science of Nature, not an Hypothesis of what Nature might be.' In this, 'the Perfection of Telescopes, and Microscopes, by which our Sense is so infinitely advanc'd, seems to be the only Way to penetrate into the most hidden Parts of Nature, and to make the most of the creation'.[67] Although Wren concealed the internal form and structure of his Cathedral, St Paul's was designed as an embodiment of the natural beauty made perceptible through such instruments, and as such was seen as a triumphant expression of the hidden truths of God's natural world.

27 East bay of south elevation, upper storey, drawn by Wren, pen, pencil and red chalk.
28 Study for upper outside transept end, drawn by Wren, pen, pencil and red chalk.
29 Wren's section through vault showing flying buttress and screen wall.
30 Wren's section through dome showing inner brick cone construction.
31 Statue of St Paul crowning the west pediment, with St Peter to the north (left) and St John to the south (right), sculpted by Francis Bird.
32 Emmanuel College chapel, Cambridge, 1668–73.
33 Trinity College library, Cambridge, 1676–84.

32

31

33

Theory into Practice: The Story of Construction

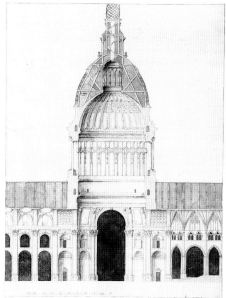

35

34

36

Old St Paul's Cathedral and Inigo Jones

The story of Wren's construction of St Paul's necessarily starts with the Old Cathedral which his building replaced. The Norman Cathedral formed the largest landmark in the medieval city, but had progressively fallen into disrepair. Following three Stuart commissions, restoration work on the Cathedral began in 1633 under the supervision of Inigo Jones. Whilst the fourteenth-century choir and eastern transept walls were merely repaired, the nave was encased with a new skin of 'antique' ornament, as were the western transept walls and their north and south facades. The transition from the magical cosmology understood by Jones to the new astronomy formulated by Wren was dramatically expressed on the site of St Paul's itself, for Jones' Ordered surface had been akin to his masque backdrops in its reflection of the harmony and proportions of Platonism.[68] Indeed Jones had featured the Cathedral itself as the focus of one of these productions, William Davenant's *Britannia Triumphans* (1638), and thereby emphasized the compatibility between his new facades and the Platonic ideals which this masque celebrated. Jones' resurfacing testifies to the symbolic importance the Stuarts attached to Old St Paul's as the spiritual centre of the reformed faith, in forming part of their plan to monumentalize London in rivalry with Rome. However, work came to a halt in September 1642 due to the Civil War, during which William Dugdale reported that the Old Cathedral had been used as a stable, with Jones' 'stately *Portico* … being converted to Shops for Seamstresses, and other Trades'.[69] As a consequence of this iconoclasm, in 1662 the Dean and Chapter had part of the choir fitted out for services whilst repairs were carried out on the main fabric.

In 1663 a Royal Commission was set up to consider the state of the Old Cathedral, and although not an original member, on his return from Paris in 1666 Wren was asked to prepare a scheme for the Cathedral's repair. Wren's 'pre-fire' scheme, as it has come to be known, involved a new dome, the replacement of the nave vaults with saucer domes and the casing of the nave itself with Corinthian pilasters. The eventual construction of a grand central space and dome was thus prefigured by Wren's intentions for the Old Cathedral. On 27 August 1666 the commissioners met at the Cathedral and John Evelyn noted in his diary Wren's plan 'to build it with a noble *Cupola*, a forme of church building, not as yet knowne in England, but of wonderfull grace … which (after much contest) was at last assented to, & that we should nominate a Committee of able Workemen to examine the present foundation'.[70]

These plans were however made redundant a month later in the wake of the Great Fire, which left most of Westminster intact but destroyed practically the whole City of London. Five days after the fire had started, on 7 September 1666 Samuel Pepys: 'Walked thence and saw all the town burned, and a miserable sight of Pauls church, with all the roofs fallen and the body of the Quire fallen into St Fayths.'[71] On the same day Evelyn found Jones' famous portico:

now rent in pieces, flakes of vast Stone Split in sunder, & nothing remaining intire but the Inscription in the *Architrave* which shewing by whom it was built, had not one letter of it defac'd … It was astonishing to see what imense stones the heate had in a manner Calcin'd, so as all the ornaments, Columns, freizes, Capitels & projectures of massie Portland stone flew off, even to the very roofe, where a Sheete of Leade covering no lesse than 6 akers by measure, being totaly mealted

37

38

... Thus lay in ashes that most venerable Church, one of the antientest Pieces of early Piety in the Christian World.[72]

Explanations for the fire ranged from the practical – a faulty baker's oven – to the conspiratorial, with Papists being accused of copying the Gunpowder plot.[73] According to one author, 'the third of September was pitched on for the Attempt, as being found by Lilly's Almanack, and a Scheme erected for that Purpose, to be a lucky Day, a Planet then ruling, which prognosticated the Downfall of Monarchy'.[74] Such reports illustrate the atmosphere of popular superstition still current in the City within which Wren's Cathedral would be raised.

The fire obviously presented a golden opportunity to remodel the whole City, an ambition which had dated from the early Stuart era. A commission was quickly appointed by both the Lord Mayor and Charles II which included Robert Hooke, Professor of Mathematics at Gresham College and a friend of Wren, and Wren himself. Of the various schemes proposed, Wren's plan – produced on 11 September, only nine days after the fire's outbreak – sought to monumentalize civic buildings such as the halls of the City Companies, the Customs House and the New Exchange by placing them at the focus of radial streets, and thereby to reconstitute the capital as an imperial city. Here Wren was reflecting the reordering of Rome by Sixtus V in 1586, whilst remaining true to the Renaissance ideal of geometric purity identified in the square grids of Roman encampments and later fortifications. Wren's views as to the social virtue of public buildings in general, which his City plan celebrated, and no doubt of the rebuilding of the Cathedral in particular, can be understood from his opening remarks of Tract I:

ARCHITECTURE has its political Use; publick Buildings being the Ornament of a Country; it establishes a Nation, draws People and Commerce; makes the People love their native Country, which Passion is the Original of all great Actions in a Common-wealth.[75]

Wren's radial streets cut through his rectangular grid forming lines of sight which applied the optical theory of light rays as outlined by Kepler and developed later by Newton. Wren's son noted that 'the Exchange [was] to stand free in the Middle of a Piazza … from whence the 60 Feet Streets as so many Rays, should proceed to all principal Parts of the City', and which in turn carried 'the Eye and Passage to the South-front of the *Exchange*'.[76] St Paul's was to be central to these views, for 'before these two Streets spreading at acute Angles, can be clear of one another, they form a triangular Piazza, the Basis of which is fill'd by the cathedral Church of St *Paul*',[77] Wren's plan was frustrated by the urgency of the need for accommodation, and the natural inclination of the citizens to return to build on old foundations. Through a Rebuilding Act of 1667, timber houses and overhanging upper storeys were outlawed, however, with the height fixed according to the importance of the street. The Act also put a tax on coal coming into the port of London which was used to compensate owners who lost land in those few improvements which were achieved, and also to finance the cost of public building works including the Cathedral.

Work on the palace at Versailles had been well under way by the time of Wren's visit in 1665, having commenced four years earlier. Whilst this would have suggested an immediate model for Wren's City, his wide radial street plan should be placed in the wider context of the emerging conception of the open, infinite universe and seen as

34 William Davenant's *Britannia Triumphans*, 1638, with St Paul's as its focus.
35 Wren's 'Pre-fire' scheme drawing for Old St Paul's.
36 Engraving of Inigo Jones' refacing from William Dugdale's *The History of St Paul's Cathedral in London*, London, 1716 ed.

37, 38 Views of Old St Paul's in the Great Fire, 1666.
39 Wren's plan for London after the Great Fire, 1666.
40 The plan for Rome by Sixtus V, 1586, from Giovanni Bordini's *De Rebus Praeclare Gestis a Sixto V Pont Max*, Rome, 1588.

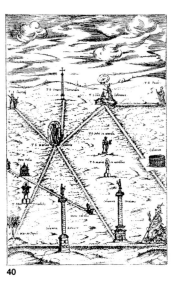

40

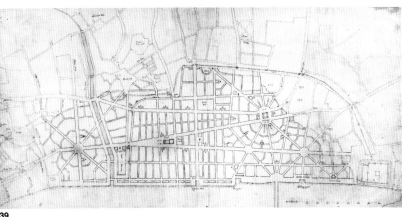

39

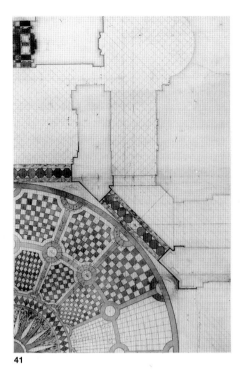

41

42

41 Wren's pavement scheme drawings, with sun inlaid in the centre under the dome.
42 The Old Cathedral after the fire as sketched by Thomas Wycke, 1666.
43, 44 Wren's model of his first Cathedral design, 1670.
45, 46 Wren's Greek cross scheme drawings.
47, 48 Wren's (Latin cross) 'Warrant design' scheme drawings.

a celebration of the sun, as the source of light and emblem of God's creation, now at the core. Indeed the eclipse of the closed model of medieval cosmology would have been powerfully symbolized in architectural terms by the destruction of the dark, narrow medieval alley pattern within the City wall and its replacement by Wren's wide streets which radiated beyond this wall. In this spirit the closed world of the medieval court would be opened up by Wren at Trinity College, Cambridge, through his external windows under the library which allowed distant views beyond Nevile's court. When accepting Gresham College's Professorship of Astronomy in 1657 Wren praised Copernicus for having guessed 'why this Body of Earth of so apt a Figure for Motion, might not move among other Celestial Bodies', and presented the dawning of the solar astronomy as an emblem of the virtues of his 'modern' age – and of Commonwealth England in particular – for he continues:

yet the apparent Absurdity of a moving Earth makes the Philosophers condemn it, tho' some of them taken with the Paradox, begin to observe Nature, and to dare to suppose some old Opinions false; and now began the first happy Appearance of Liberty to Philosophy, oppress'd by the Tyranny of the *Greek* and *Roman* Monarchies.'[78]

In this speech Wren cast London as an astronomical city blessed by the Copernican heavens, 'a City particularly favour'd by the Celestial Influences, a *Pandora*, on which each Planet hath contributed something'; here 'the Sun looks most benignly on it, for, what City in the World so vastly populous, doth yet enjoy so healthy an Air, so fertile a Soil?'[79] As a temple celebrating the dawning of this new age of enlightenment, Wren's pale gold Portland stone Cathedral, when

imagined in the context of his unrealized city, stood at a centre in the radial pattern as a metaphorical source of 'light'. A luminous interior was created with clear glass windows and vaults of plaster and gold paintwork,[80] unlike the atmosphere of the medieval Cathedral but imitating the Temple of Peace which, according to Wren, as 'a Hall of Justice … was made very lightsome; whereas the consecrated Temples were generally very obscure'.[81] In echoing the traditional identification of Christ with Apollo, the new Copernican astronomy was most explicitly celebrated by Wren's golden sun inlaid in the marble pavement at the very centre of the Cathedral under the dome, itself a traditional symbol for the 'sky-dome' or heavens. Indeed, the 365 feet from ground level to the top of the dome's cross obviously reflects the astronomical year – that is, the earth's annual rotation around the sun.

The circle and the cross:
Wren's early designs for St Paul's Cathedral

Despite Evelyn's dramatic report, the Old Cathedral was not completely destroyed in the Great Fire, with parts of the nave walls and Jones' portico left standing. For three years following the fire, the site was cleared of melted lead, the vaulted roof and walls were taken down and the floors dug up with a view to reusing the surviving parts of the old building, held as it was in great esteem. In January 1668 the commission for rebuilding the City ordered that a temporary choir with altar and pulpit be fitted out in the west end, but later that year the unsoundness of the structure finally became apparent and a new building was resolved upon. The state of the fabric was relayed to Wren in Oxford by the Cathedral Dean, William Sancroft, who wrote on 25 April 1668:

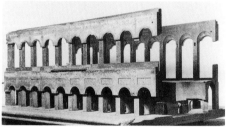

43

44

Our Work at the West-end of St *Paul's* is fallen about our Ears. Your quick Eye discern'd the Walls and Pillars gone off from their Perpendiculars, and I believe other Defects too, which are now expos'd to every common Observer … The second Pillar (which you know is bigger than the rest) stands now alone, with an enormous Weight on the Top of it; which we cannot hope should stand long, and yet we dare not venture to take it down.

It was out of this structural impasse that Wren's commission arose, for Sancroft ended his account by asking: 'What we are to do next is the present Deliberation, in which you are so absolutely and indispensably necessary to us, that we can do nothing, resolve on nothing, without you.' Sancroft adds that: 'You will think fit, I know, to bring with you those excellent Draughts and Designs you formerly favour'd us with.'[82] A Royal Warrant was issued on 15 July 1668 for the final demolition and clearance of the choir and tower, 'in such manner as shall be judged sufficient to make room for a new Choir, of a faire and decent fabrick neare or upon the old foundations'.[83]

Although not officially architect of St Paul's until 1673, Wren's first design for the Cathedral followed his appointment as Surveyor of the King's Works in 1669, and is preserved in a wooden model constructed some time before June 1670. This design, the first ever for an English Protestant Cathedral, comprised a rectangular hall with ground floor loggias and, at the west end, a square vestibule for ceremonial surmounted by a dome. In this somewhat strange arrangement Wren clearly reassembled the elements in his small plan sketched on the City layout of 1666. In *Parentalia* Wren's son probably recorded the feelings of his father in noting that before the allocation of money from the tax on sea-coal, 'it seemed in vain in

any new Designs, to propose an Edifice too large and costly'. Accordingly Wren was 'at first directed to contrive a Fabrick of moderate Bulk, but of good Proportion; a convenient Quire, with a Vestibule, and Porticoes, and a Dome conspicuous above the Houses'. However the design met with opposition since, according to Wren's son, 'being contriv'd in the *Roman* Stile, was not so well understood and relish'd by others, who thought it deviated too much from the old *Gothick* Form of cathedral Churches, which they had been used to see and admire in this Country'.[84] Wren's proposal thus fell victim to the love of customary beauty and as such may have formed a direct context for his strictures in the Tracts.

The design was duly abandoned and on 12 November 1673 Charles II issued a long commission for rebuilding St Paul's in which he commended a design by Wren for a Cathedral with a Greek cross plan, dome and giant Corinthian portico the size and form of which was clearly intended to rival that of the Pantheon, praised by Wren in Tract III as 'a Coloss-work, and most wonderfully rich'.[85] In approving the design, the King instructed 'a Model thereof to be made after so large and exact a manner, that it may remain as a perpetual and unchangeable rule and direction for the conduct of the whole Work'.[86] This 'Great Model' cost over £500 and represents a design said by Wren's son to be the Surveyor's favourite. Wren was forced to abandon it, however, partly since it was impossible to construct in stages, as funds dictated, but principally because the clergy favoured the customary, medieval Latin cross form which expressed a continuity with the medieval Church and gave a separate choir necessary for traditional services. Wren's son recorded that 'the Clergy thought the Model not enough of a Cathedral-fashion',[87] thereby echoing the objections to the first scheme, although this

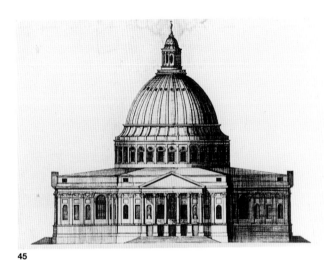

45

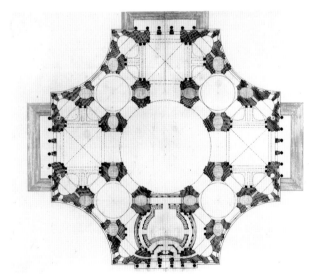

46

47

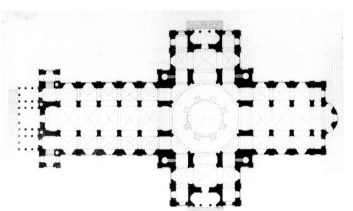

48

49

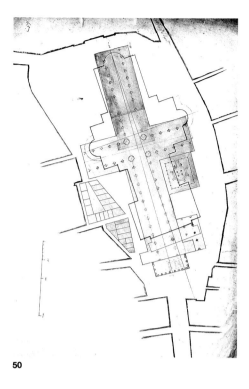

50

centralized design was obviously more pure in geometric terms in its reflection of Wren's principle of natural beauty. Such tension between beauty and convenience was expressed elsewhere in Wren's City churches, and the constant attempt to reconcile a centralized structure with longitudinal plan.

This led to a third scheme, Wren's 'Warrant design', so-called after the Royal approval granted on 14 May 1675.[88] This combined twin domes surmounted by a tall spire with a Latin cross plan in seeking, as his son noted, 'to reconcile, as near as possible, the *Gothick* to a better Manner of Architecture'.[89] From now on this remained a consistent aim, although the design became merely the first stage in the evolution of the building itself and of Wren's attempt to reconcile the customary practices imposed on him with his desire for natural beauty outlined in the Tracts. Henceforth his son adds that 'the *Surveyor* resolved to make no more Models, or publickly expose his Drawings, which, (as he had found by Experience,) did but lose Time, and subjected his Business many Times, to incompetent Judges'.[90] A comparison between the Warrant design and the Cathedral itself shows the extent to which Wren made use of the King's permission to 'make some Variations, rather ornamental, than essential, as from Time to Time he should see proper'.[91] The Cathedral was indeed constructed without the normal aid of a wooden model and, with much of the building wrapped in scaffolding, few besides the architect had any idea of its complex design. However, since any site work necessarily prefigures the later structure, the final design must have been well advanced before the first building contracts were confirmed just two months following the Warrant, that is by July 1675, but how Wren achieved this remains something of a mystery.[92] The key change from the Warrant plan was the reduction of the nave

from five bays to three, thereby balancing the three bays of the choir and reflecting the earlier, centrally planned model. Clearly the intention of the Warrant design for a spire growing from the dome was also abandoned in this movement towards the purification of the Cathedral's form.

From foundation to dome: the building of St Paul's Cathedral
Demolition of the Old Cathedral, begun in 1668, proved unusually difficult as the stonework had been bonded by molten lead. To overcome this, the fruits of the mathematical sciences were applied by Wren, for he used gunpowder (and, when this proved dangerous, a battering ram) to clear the most massive remains of the central tower: a year earlier he had reported to the Royal Society on his experiments on the force of gunpowder in lifting weights and bending springs.[93] Pepys noted the progress of the demolition in his diary for 26 August 1668: 'it is strange to see with what speed the people imployed do pull down Paul's steeple – and with what ease. It is said that it and the Quire are to be taken down this year, and another church begun in the room thereof the next'.[94] On 14 September he further observed that it was 'strange how the very sight of the stones falling from the top of the steeple doth make me sea-sick',[95] and two days later again visited the site:

and do see a hideous sight, of the walls of the church ready to fall, that I was in fear as long as I was in it. And here I saw the great vaults underneath the body of the church. No hurt, I hear, is done yet, since their going to pull down the church and steeple; but one man, on Monday this week, fell from the top to a piece of the roof of the east end that stands next the steeple, and there broke himself all to pieces.[96]

49 Wren's definitive design (1675), south elevation.
50 Wren's drawing of the realignment of the Cathedral.

51, 52 Details of the choir at St Paul's with decorative carvings by Grinling Gibbons on the organ case (51) and choir stalls (52).
53 Details of interior and exterior stone carving drawn by Arthur Poley, published in *St Paul's Cathedral, London, Measured, Drawn and Described*, London, 1927.

51

52

INTERNAL DETAILS

1 PILASTERS TO TRANSEPT WINDOWS
  AND WINDOWS AT WEST END.
2 COFFER TO MAIN ARCHES.
3 MAIN VAULTING TO NAVE & CHANCEL.
4 SOFFIT OF MAIN ARCHES.
5 SOFFIT OF TRANSEPT ARCHES.
6 CONSOLE TO CLERESTORY WINDOWS.
7 KEYSTONE UNDER WHISPERING GALLERY.
8 KEYSTONE UNDER WHISPERING GALLERY.
9 KEYSTONE UNDER WHISPERING " (SIDE).
10 MAIN ENTABLATURE & CAPITAL.
11 BARREL VAULTS TO AISLES &
   UPPER PART OF ORDER.

EXTERNAL DETAILS.

12,13,14, VASES ON WESTERN TOWERS.
15, ENTABLATURE OF CORINTHIAN ORDER.
16, ARCHITRAVE & SILL TO AISLE WINDOWS.

ST. PAUL'S CATHEDRAL, LONDON.
DETAILS OF STONE CARVINGS

BALUSTRADE

53

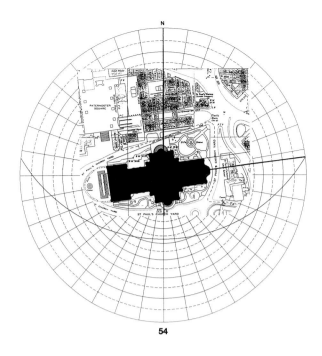

54

55

56

Wren's resolution to build on new foundations dated from the first design, since the old foundations obviously embodied the Gothic Cathedral's ground plan and structure, but his decision to rotate the new Cathedral further from true east is more puzzling. According to the architect's son, there was more space to the northeast of the site,[97] although Wren's building would appear to have in fact moved further southwest through being rotated about the easternmost point of the Old Cathedral. It has also been suggested that a change of axis was necessary to bring the centre of the west front in line with the planned approach,[98] although this evidently would not have been the case if Wren's plan of 1666 had been realized, and the rotation has in fact further distorted the relationship with Fleet Street as built. Echoing the sun emblem set in the pavement at the centre of this axis, it is more likely that astronomical factors were used by the Professor Emeritus of Astronomy to fix the otherwise arbitrary rotation from true east and the setting out of St Paul's with respect to the heavens. For the Cathedral is aligned with the point on the horizon of sunrise on 4 April,[99] which coincides with the date of Easter on the year of foundation, 1675.[100] Wren certainly knew the astronomical declination of the Cathedral, for he had intended to use St Paul's as an observatory.[101] Hence the architect-astronomer united the most important date of the Christian calendar, the day of Christ's resurrection, with the new sun-centred astronomy in orientating his great temple, which had itself been resurrected from the ashes of the old. An indication of this intention, together with the superstition surrounding the Cathedral and its centre (later decorated with the solar emblem), is recorded by Wren's son in the form of a famous anecdote:

In the Beginning of the new Works of St *Paul's*, an Incident was taken notice of by some People as a memorable Omen, when the *Surveyor* in Person had set out, upon the Place, the Dimensions of the great Dome, and fixed upon the Centre; a common Labourer was ordered to bring a flat Stone from the Heaps of Rubbish, (such as should first come to Hand) to be laid for a Mark and Direction to the Masons; the Stone which was immediately brought and laid down for that purpose, happened to be a Piece of a Grave-Stone, with nothing remaining of the Inscription but the single Word in large Capitals, RESURGAM.[102]

This word appears in a block set into the Cathedral's south transept pediment, underneath a carving by Caius Gabriel Cibber of a sunburst framing a phoenix, the solar fire bird and itself a symbol of resurrection. The foundation stone, which was the first element to embody the new alignment and which tradition records was laid by Charles II,[103] was set in the Cathedral's southeast corner – that is, facing sunrise: Elias Ashmole, the astrologer and Royal Society fellow, noted this ceremony in his diary as the 25 June 1675 at the curious time of 6.30 am.[104] This was two weeks after the summer solstice (St Barnabas' Day) and, as one of the longest days of the year,[105] was perhaps thought auspicious for the Cathedral's foundation. As an indication of such superstitions surrounding building foundation, John Flamsteed, the Astronomer Royal, calculated a horoscope on the 10 August of that year for the founding of Wren's Greenwich Observatory.[106]

The Work's Accounts[107] record the enormity of the Cathedral site work, involving the coordination of labourers for digging and laying foundations, carpenters for building scaffolding and centring, brick-layers and plasterers for the crypt vaults, masons for setting the stone-work, plumbers for leadwork to the roofs, joiners for making models of

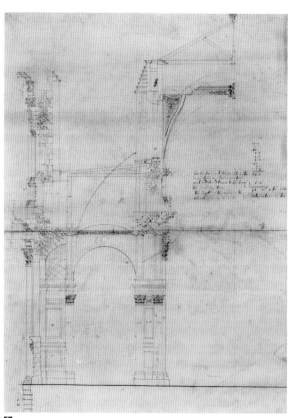

57

details and carvers for sculpting these, which were in turn protected by carpenters' casings. Portland stone from Dorset was used for the exterior, the most durable material in London's smoky conditions. This stone had to be transported by sea to the port of London, unloaded into barges which could pass below London Bridge on their way to Paul's Wharf, from where the stone was carted to the site. Throughout the progress of the work various masons were contracted to build specific parts of the Cathedral. On 18 June 1675 contracts were signed with two masons for work on the choir foundations and crypt piers: the first, Joshua Manshall, was Master Mason to the King; the other, Thomas Strong, owned stone quarries near Oxford. The Cathedral occupied a number of men for most of their working lives: John Oliver (c1616–1701), for example, one of the surveyors appointed by the commission for rebuilding the City churches, became Deputy-Surveyor in 1676 and remained on the work until his death, aged 85.

Whilst the Royal Warrant had clearly instructed that the Cathedral should be built in phases starting with the choir, with the choir walls having reached a height of 10 feet,[108] as early as March 1676 contracts were signed for the southwest and northwest 'peer or leg of the Dome'.[109] Extension of the foundations to the two transepts began on 9 November 1676 and, two years later, work commenced on the exterior of the south transept. Foundations for the nave were begun on 5 September 1678 and by 1684 Thomas Strong's younger brother, Edward, was working on the walls to the north side of the nave. Progress on site was thus remarkably rapid. A contract to carve the great cornice inside the choir was issued in early 1685, and by April of that year the choir walls, including the side aisles and great arched vaults in the crypt, were finished, as were the new Chapter house, vestries, two transept porticoes and the eight huge pillars supporting the dome. Work began on the west end in August 1688. By September 1694 the masonry of the choir was completed, and John Evelyn praised the work in his diary entry for 5 October:

I went to Paules to see the Choire now finished, as to the stone work & that part both without & within the scaffolds struck: some exceptions might yet perhaps be taken without as the placing Columns upon Pilasters, at the East Tribunal: As to the rest certainly a piece of Architecture without reproch: The pulling out of the Formes, like drawers from under the stalles, is very ingenious.[110]

The choir fittings remained to be installed, and this task united the work of many leading craftsmen; Jean Tijou supplied the iron gates forming the original choir screen, Bernard Smith made the organ, whilst Grinling Gibbons carved cornucopia and flowers in panels originally set in the old organ case and wreaths in the oak screens to the rear of the choir stalls, all Arcadian motifs traditionally signifying a renewed Golden Age. Echoing this theme, Gibbons also carved the cherubim and flora below the great round-headed windows, and Francis Bird carved the relief depicting the conversion of St Paul in the pediment surmounting the portico. The choir was opened on 2 December 1697 and three days later Evelyn noted:

Was the first Sonday, St Paules had had any service in it, since it was Consumed at the Conflagration of the Citty; 1666: which I my selfe saw, & now was likewise my selfe there, the Quire being compleatly finished, & the Organ esteemed the best in Europe of I think 40 stops; There were the Bishop of Lond, Lord Major & innumerable multitude, one Mr Knight preaching (for Dr Sherlock the Deane).[111]

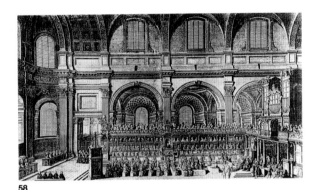

58

59

60

61

62

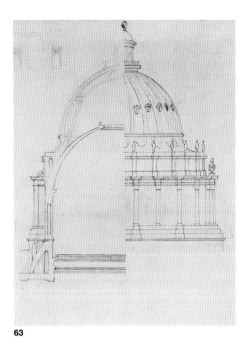

63   64

65   66

The west towers were built between 1705 and 1708 by two masons, the northern by Samuel Fulkes and the southern by William Kempster, whilst the west end was roofed at about the same time. Last to be completed was work on the portico (in 1706) and, with the structure having reached whispering gallery level in 1698, the construction of the dome. Various drawings record the evolution of the dome's design, the second largest after St Peter's in Rome and unprecedented in England. A model was made in December 1706 and the work itself progressed such that in April 1708 tarred cloth was erected 'to cover the workmen in hot & wet weather upon the Leading ye Roofe of the Dome'.[112] Wren followed the design of the dome of St Peter's in using iron chains as girdles, noting in Tract II that since this 'was hooped with Iron, it is safe at present, and, without an Earthquake, for Ages to come. Iron, at all Adventures, is a good Caution'.[113] In the new spirit of experimentation, Wren invented a system of scaffolding for the building of this inner brick cone. The architect's son records that:

The Concave was turned upon a Centre; which … was laid without any Standards from below to support it; and as it was both Centering and Scaffolding, it remained for the Use of the Painter. Every Story of this Scaffolding being circular, and the Ends of all the Ledgers meeting as so many Rings, and truly wrought, it supported itself. This Machine was an Original of the Kind, and will be a useful Project for the like Work to an Architect hereafter.[114]

The Cathedral was finished in 1710 having cost, according to the final accounts, £738,845 5s 21/2d. Wren continued to be involved with the Cathedral's fitting out up to his death on 25 February 1723, but had

by then become increasingly alienated by the younger generation who had taken charge of his masterpiece, and in particular by William Benson who had replaced him as Surveyor in 1718. The old man, aged about 85, reacted strongly against the decision to top the Cathedral with a balustrade: this was evidence once again of the great error of customary beauty, people expecting, as he put it, 'something they had been used to in Gothic structures'.[115]

Wren's new St Peter's
Wren and his contemporaries at the Royal Society saw their era as a renewal of the Golden Age of antiquity which had characterized the rule of Augustus,[116] an identification underlined by the advantages flowing from the Royal Society, the restored and reformed constitutional monarchy and restored aspiration to beauty in holiness originally sponsored by the pre-Civil War Church of England. Baroque High Church ornamentation at St Paul's coincided with a period of Catholic toleration which was epitomized by the rule of the Catholic James II (1685–8). Wren's St Paul's was, however, the first Protestant Cathedral and through its ornamentation and form represented an attempt to formulate an architectural style suitable for Protestant worship some 150 years after the original split with Rome. This search for identity was characterized in particular through rivalry in the popular imagination with the principal temple of the Catholic Church, St Peter's in Rome. In this spirit, one of the 1663 commissioners advising on the repair of the Old Cathedral, Sir Roger Pratt, in 'St Paul's and the New Way of Architecture for Churches' of 1672 claimed that St Peter's 'could hardly if at all be brought to suit with such and so old a body as our Pauls'.[117] In reflecting this aspiration Wren's dome design adapted that of Bramante for

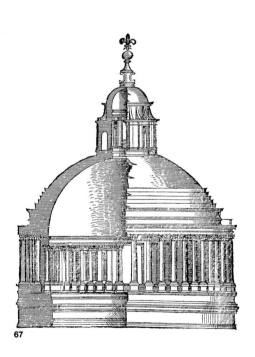

67

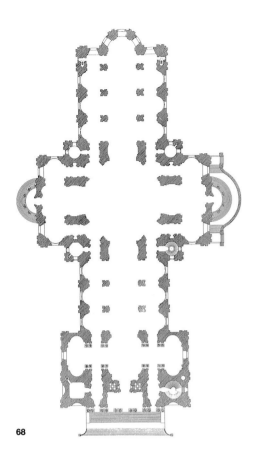

68

St Peter's, as illustrated by Serlio (III fol 66v) and studied in Tract II,[118] whilst Wren's design for the Baldacchino with its twisted columns clearly reflected Bernini's masterpiece in the Catholic temple. The first volume of Colen Campbell's *Vitruvius Britannicus* published three years after the Cathedral's completion, in 1715–7, opened with illustrations of St Paul's followed by those of St Peter's to demonstrate the British temple's superiority. Indeed in *Parentalia*, Wren's son made much of the rivalry between the two Corinthian churches, since St Peter's was, compared to St Paul's, 'the only Edifice that can come in Competition with it'.[119] But whereas St Peter's had taken over 145 years to build, and involved no less than 12 architects, St Paul's had been built in a mere 35 years to the design of just one man, his father, Sir Christopher Wren.

When Edward Wright visited St Peter's in the early 1720s he observed that whilst 'the Parts are certainly very beautiful',

the Whole is terminated by a strait Line at top, which (without any prejudice in favour of my own Country) I cannot think has so good an effect as the agreeable variety, which is given by the Turrets at each end, and the Pediment rising in the middle, of the front of S *Paul's*.[120]

Such praise echoed Wren's own optical design criteria, and indeed it is ultimately as a triumph of his principle of natural beauty over customary constraints that St Paul's should be understood. Just as the new 'experimental' philosophy adapted and retained certain established concepts, so the Cathedral is testimony to Wren's capacity to overcome and utilize traditional Gothic and Renaissance practices within his fundamental re-examination of architectural principles. His life spanned the transition from the Renaissance,

Platonic conception of nature represented in the work of Inigo Jones, to the revival in the 1720s of Jones' restrained architecture by the 'Palladians' under Colen Campbell, Lord Burlington and William Kent. Now, shorn of Renaissance cosmology in reflecting the so-called Age of Reason, this revival of the Vitruvian rules and celebration of Jones as the *Vitruvius Britannicus* represented a reaction to, as Campbell put it, the 'excessive Ornaments without Grace'[121] of continental Baroque. Wren was himself hailed as a Vitruvian by Campbell whilst attacked for breaking with tradition by more fundamental 'Ancients'. As such, the publication of *Parentalia* in 1750 was an attempt to defend Wren's reputation and the theories behind his architecture, and coincided with the celebration by Canaletto of the British architect's work as a worthy rival to the glories of Venice.

In the first of his Tracts Wren advised the architect 'to think his Judges, as well those that are to live five Centuries after him, as those of his own Time'.[122] If St Paul's Cathedral failed to cast in stone enduring, absolute principles of architecture as had been hoped, it would certainly immortalize its creator. Wren's epitaph set in the centre of the solar pavement includes the words 'Si Monumentum Requiris, Circumspice' – 'If you seek his monument, look around you'. John Evelyn in his dedication of *An Account of Architects and Architecture* (1706) placed Wren's Cathedral at the centre of the new astronomy when he eulogized:

… you need no *Panegyric*, or other *History* to Eternize them, than the *greatest City* of the *Universe*, which You have *Rebuilt* and *Beautified*, and are still improving: Witness the *Churches*, the Royal *Courts*, Stately *Halls*, *Magazines*, *Palaces*, and other Publick Structures … that if the whole *Art* of *Building* were lost, it might be *Recover'd* and *found* again in St *Paul's*.

63 Wren's drawing showing the evolution of the design of the dome.
64 Isometric of the Cathedral showing construction, drawn by R B Brook-Greaves and W Godfrey Allen.
65 Detail of the southwest clock tower: William Kempster was the mason and Francis Bird the sculptor.
66 The clock on the south-west tower.
67 Serlio's illustration of Bramante's dome for St Peter's (III fol 66v).

68, 69, 70 St Paul's in the first volume of Colen Campbell's *Vitruvius Britannicus*, London, 1715–7, with the plan and west front shown in comparison with St Peter's in Rome (fig 70).
71 St Paul's in the context of the City churches, panorama by the Buck brothers, 1749.
72 (overleaf) St Paul's and Wren's church steeples by Canaletto, *Thames from Somerset House*, 1751–2.

71

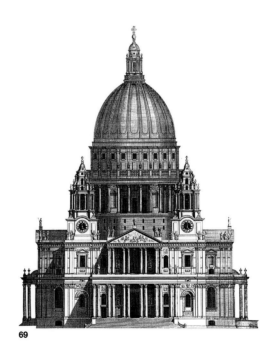

69

70

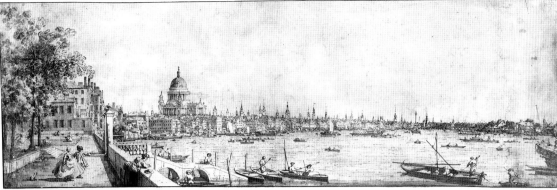

72

Notes

General note: The spelling and italicization of words in the quotations replicate those in the original sources.

1 See Hart, V, *Art and Magic in the Court of the Stuarts* (London: Routledge, 1994).

2 See Thomas, K, *Religion and the Decline of Magic*, (London: Weidenfeld and Nicolson / Penguin, 1971).

3 See Tract V, in Bolton, A T, and H P Hendry (eds), *Wren Society Publications*, vol xix (1924–43), p 141, which cites the legendary musical magic of Amphion. For Wren's faith in dream prophecy see Wren, S, *Parentalia: Or, Memoirs of the Family of the Wrens* (1750), p 348, quoting Aubrey, J, *Miscellanies* (1696), p 52.

4 See Hunter, M, *Science and Society in Restoration England* (Cambridge University Press, 1981).

5 Perrault, C, *Ordonnance des cinq espèces de colonnes* (1683); Fréart de Chambray, R, *Parallèle de l'Architecture antique et de la moderne* (1650): see Rykwert, J, *The First Moderns* (Cambridge MA and London: MIT Press, 1980), pp 148–9; Bennett, J A, *The Mathematical Sciences of Christopher Wren* (Cambridge University Press, 1982), pp 122–3; Harris, E, *British Architectural Books and Writers 1556–1785* (Cambridge University Press, 1990), pp 368–71, pp 505–6.

6 In Wren, S, *op cit*, p 356.

7 *Ibid*, p 200.

8 Wren's interest in these is attested by his library. See Watkin, D J (ed), *'Architects': Sale Catalogues of Libraries of Eminent Persons* (1972): the list includes 'Busbequius's Travels' (lot 157: p 15); 'Perier's Voyages and Travels – Voyage to Constantinople 1699' (lot 207: p 19); 'Voyage d'Italie, de Grèce, & du Levant, Par Spon, 1679' (lot 318: p 24); 'Pencet's Voyage to Ethiopia'; 'Dampier's Voyage to Holland' (lot 439: p 31); 'Ogilby's Description of Africa, 1679' (lot 539: p 36).

9 Tract V, in Bolton, A T, and H P Hendry, *op cit*, vol XIX, p 140.

10 In Wren, S, *op cit*, Tract I, p 351; Tract II, p 354.

11 On this see Rykwert, J, *On Adam's House in Paradise; The Idea of the Primitive Hut in Architectural History* (New York: Museum of Modern Art Papers on Architecture and MIT Press, 1972).

12 In Wren, S, *op cit*, p 353.

13 See Rykwert, J, *The First Modern*, pp 30–9, pp 48–9, and Harris, E, *op cit*, pp 368–9.

14 In Wren, S, *op cit*, p 353.

15 *Ibid*, p 288.

16 *Ibid*, p 355.

17 *Ibid*.

18 The Corinthian columns were famed for their four-foot module, cited as such in the commentary to St Paul's in Colen Campbell's *Vitruvius Britannicus* (1715–17).

19 In Wren, S, *op cit*, p 360.

20 *Ibid*, p 351.

21 *Ibid*, p 360. See Villalpando, J B, *In Ezechielem Explanationes et Apparatus Urbis ac Templi Hierosolymitani*, iii vols, (Rome, 1596–1604).

22 Evelyn, J, *A Parallel of the Ancient Architecture with the Modern* (1664), p 76.

23 In Wren, S, *op cit*, p 366.

24 *Ibid*, p 362.

25 Wren owned Kircher's *Ars Magna Lucis & Umbrae* (Amsterdam, 1671) and *Phonurgia Nova*, Campidano, (1673 ed); see Watkin, D J, *op cit*, lots 244, 247 (p 20).

26 See Bolton, A T, and H P Hendry, *op cit*, vol XIX, p 140.

27 See Koyré, A, *From the Closed World to the Infinite Universe* (Baltimore: Johns Hopkins University Press, 1968); Webster, C, *From Paracelsus to Newton, Magic and the Making of Modern Science* (Cambridge University Press, 1982); Koestler, A, *The Sleepwalkers* (London: Hutchinson, 1959).

28 Discussed by Bennett, J A, *op cit*, pp 2–3.

29 In Wren, S, *op cit*, p 261.

30 *Ibid*, p 351.

31 *Ibid*, p 359.

32 *Ibid*, p 357.

33 Greaves, J, *A Description of the grand Signor's Seraglio, or Turkish Emperours Court* (London, 1650).

34 In Wren, S, *op cit*, p 291.

35 *Ibid*, p 290.

36 *Ibid*, p 362.

37 See Addleshaw, G, Etchells, F, *The Architectural Setting of Anglican Worship* (London: Faber and Faber, 1948), pp 52–6.

38 In Wren, S, *op cit*, p 320.

39 *Ibid*, p 363.

40 *Ibid*, p 362.

41 *Ibid*, p 306.

42 Wren to Dean Sancroft, 24 November 1666: see Bolton, A T, and H P Hendry, *op cit*, vol XIII, p 45.

43 In Wren, S, *op cit*, p 289.

44 *Ibid*, p 363.

45 *Ibid*, p 351.

46 *Ibid*, p 275.

47 *Ibid*, p 356.

48 *Ibid*, p 351.

49 From the English translation by John James of Perrault's *Ordonnance*, published as *A Treatise of the Five Orders of Columns* (1708), p x. See Rykwert, J, *op cit*, pp 148–9; Harris, E, *op cit*, pp 368–71, pp 505–506.

50 In Wren, S, *op cit*, p 352.

51 *Ibid*, p 366.

52 *Ibid*, p 365.

53 *Ibid*, p 351.

54 *Ibid*, p 352.

55 See Fréart de Chambray, *op cit*: trans by Evelyn, J, *op cit*, see Preface, p 3; discussed by Bennett, J A, *op cit*, p 123.

56 In Wren, S, *op cit*, p 352.

57 *Ibid*.

58 *Ibid*, p 276.

59 *Ibid*, p 288

60 *Ibid*, p 353.

61 *Ibid*, p 321.

62 *Ibid*, p 352.

63 *Ibid*, p 356.

64 *Ibid*, p 352.

65 *Ibid*, p 353.

66 *Ibid*, p 291.

67 *Ibid*, pp 204–5.

68 See Hart, V, *op cit*.

69 Dugdale, W, *The History of St Paul's Cathedral in London* (1716 ed), p 305.

70 Evelyn, J, *Diary* (ed E S De Beer) (Oxford University Press and London, 1959), p 494.

71 Pepys, S, *Diary* (ed R Latham, W Matthews) (London: Bell and Hyman, 1970–83), vol 7, p 279.

72 Evelyn, J, *op cit*, p 498.

73 See Bedloe, W, *A Narrative and Impartial Discovery of the Horrid Popish Plot* (London, 1679).

74 Anon, possibly Sir T Herbert, in Dugdale, W, *op cit*, p 152.

75 In Wren, S, *op cit*, p 351.

76 *Ibid*, p 268.

77 *Ibid*.

78 *Ibid*, p 204.

79 *Ibid*, p 206.

80 The gold paintwork in the dome, and gold decoration such as Tijou's iron gates now between the aisles and high altar are original. The gold mosaics in the choir domes and central dome replaced the plaster between 1863–92, added by Dr Salviati of Venice.

81 In Wren, S, *op cit*, p 362.

82 *Ibid*, pp 278–9.

83 See Bolton, A T, and H P Hendry, *op cit*, vol XIII, p 23.

84 In Wren, S, *op cit*, pp 281–2.

85 *Ibid*, p 359.

86 See Bolton, A T, and H P Hendry, *op cit*, vol XIII, p 27.

87 In Wren, S, *op cit*, p 282.

88 State Papers (Domestic), 14 May 1675, pp 118–9.

89 In Wren, S, *op cit*, p 282.

90 *Ibid*, p 283.

91 *Ibid*.

92 For a discussion of this see Downes, K, *Sir Christopher Wren: The Design of St Paul's Cathedral* (London: Trefoil, 1988), pp 18–21.

93 See the *Dictionary of National Biography* (Oxford University Press and London, 1937 ed), entry for Wren, p 998.

94 Pepys, S, *op cit*, vol 9, p 288.

95 *Ibid*, p 305.

96 *Ibid*, pp 307–8.

97 In Wren, S, *op cit*, p 287.

98 See Bolton, A T, and H P Hendry, *op cit*, vol XIII, pp xi–xii.

99 Declination of 4.34 degrees; latitude of 51.52 degrees north. The date of sunrise corresponding to the Cathedral alignment was calculated by Martin Wilkinson, lecturer in lighting in the School of Architecture and Building Engineering, Bath University.

100 In England Easter was celebrated on 4 April (Julian, old style calender) in 1675 (see almanac Cambridge University Library, Tab.b.561[51]). The date of solar alignment for the Cathedral is however calculated against the astronomically correct Gregorian (new style) year, which had been used on the continent since 1582. In the old style calendar, used in England until 1752, the vernal equinox which determined Easter had slipped ten days from its correct date (21 March, new style). Given this inaccuracy, Wren can be seen to have taken the date of Easter (old style) for 1675 and calculated the sunrise for that date in the correct (new style) calendar. Easter limits are 22 March to 25 April (new style), and so 4 April falls approximately mid-way within this cycle.

101 See Bennett, J A, *op cit*, p 42.

102 In Wren, S, *op cit*, p 292.

103 See Conder, E, 'King Charles II at the Royal Exchange, London in 1667', *Ars Quatuor Coronatorum*, vol xi (1898), p 145.

104 See Ashmole, E, *Elias Ashmole (1617–1692), His Autobiographical and Historical Notes* (ed C H Josten), vol iv (Oxford University Press, 1966), p 1432.

105 From the almanac for 1675, *op cit*.

106 Conder, E, *op cit*, p 144.

107 See Bolton, A T, and H P Hendry, *op cit*, vols XIII–XVI, XVIII–IXX.

108 State Papers (Domestic), 3 March 1676, p 5.

109 See Bolton, A T, and H P Hendry, *op cit*, vol XIII, p 86.

110 Evelyn, J, *op cit*, p 987.

111 *Ibid*, p 1020.

112 See Bolton, A T, and H P Hendry, *op cit*, vol XV, p 162.

113 In Wren, S, *op cit*, p 356.

114 *Ibid*, p 291.

115 In Bolton, A T, and H P Hendry, *op cit*, vol XVI, pp 130–1.

116 Discussed in Bennett, J A, *op cit*, p 117.

117 See Pratt, R, *The Architecture of Sir Roger Pratt* (ed R T Gunther), (Oxford University Press, 1928), p 196.

118 In Wren, S, *op cit*, p 356.

119 *Ibid*, p 293; see also pp 287–92.

120 Wright, E, *Some Observations Made in Travelling through France, Italy etc* in The Years 1720, 1721 and 1722, vol 1 (London, 1730), p 206.

121 Campbell, C, *op cit*, 'Introduction'.

122 In Wren, S, *op cit*, p 352.

Left The upper, paired
Composite columns of the
unique two-tier west portico,
one of the last elements to
be completed in 1706. The
pediment carries a relief
depicting St Paul's
conversion, crowned with a
statue of St Paul flanked by
that of St Peter on the north
(left) and St John on the
south (right), all carved by
Francis Bird.
Right Detail of the portico
on the west front.

Opposite The Cathedral dome was the second largest after St Peter's in Rome and was an unprecedented form of roof construction in England. A model was made in December 1706 and the work itself progressed to such an extent that in April 1708 tarred cloth was erected to cover the workmen in hot and wet weather. Wren invented a system of scaffolding for the building of the inner brick cone, and for stability he used iron chains as girdles made by Jean Tijou.

The cross was designed in 1708 and is 365 feet above ground level.

Above The northwest bell tower.

Right Details of the southwest clock tower.

Left and above The south transept pediment with the phoenix and sunburst carved by Caius Gabriel Cibber. The idea of resurrection, which the Cathedral symbolizes, is here emphasized by the word 'Resurgam'.

Wren, aged about 85, reacted strongly against the decision to top the Cathedral walls with a balustrade: this was evidence of the great error of what he defined as customary beauty, people expecting, as he put it, 'something they had been used to in Gothic structures'.
Right Detail of the north facade at the western end.

Left Detail of the south transept pediment. At roof level Wren applied his principle that: 'No sort of Pinnacle is worthy enough to appear in the Air, but Statue. Pyramids are *Gothick*.'
Right Detail of the south transept facade.

Far left Detail of the south transept facade.

Left and above left Details of the bas-relief panels under the windows carved by Grinling Gibbons, 1694–5, both at the east end. Wren used these Arcadian motifs to signify a renewed Golden Age.

Above Detail of the apse at the east end, viewed from the south. In praising the antique Temple of Mars Ultor Wren comments that 'a Semicircle joining to an Oblong, as in the Tribunal at the End of this Temple, is a graceful Composition'.

Left The south transept portico.
Right The north facade of the Cathedral, at the base of the tower at the west end, with the paired Corinthian pilasters which order the lower storey of St Paul's.

Left Interior of the Cathedral looking east down the three bays of the nave. Following his reappraisal of architectural development to include newly discovered monuments and styles, Wren commended structural techniques drawn from Byzantine architecture in advising: 'you may build upon that Circle an upright Wall, which may bear a Cupola again above, as is done at *St Sophia*'. He made clear his use of this system 'in the vaulting of the Church of *St Paul's*'.

Right View of the nave. Wren based his arrangement of the pilasters and arches on that in the Roman Temple of Peace (Basilica of Maxentius).

Left The central crossing under the dome, looking east towards the pulpit and organ, with a glimpse of the south transept through the arch.

Right The dome, with view through to the lantern and detail of the fresco painted by Sir James Thornhill, 1716–9, against Wren's wishes.

Far left Detail of one of the saucer domes in the aisles.
Left and above Decorative details in the nave. Acanthus decoration on a pilaster base in the clerestory under the lesser dome at the west end.

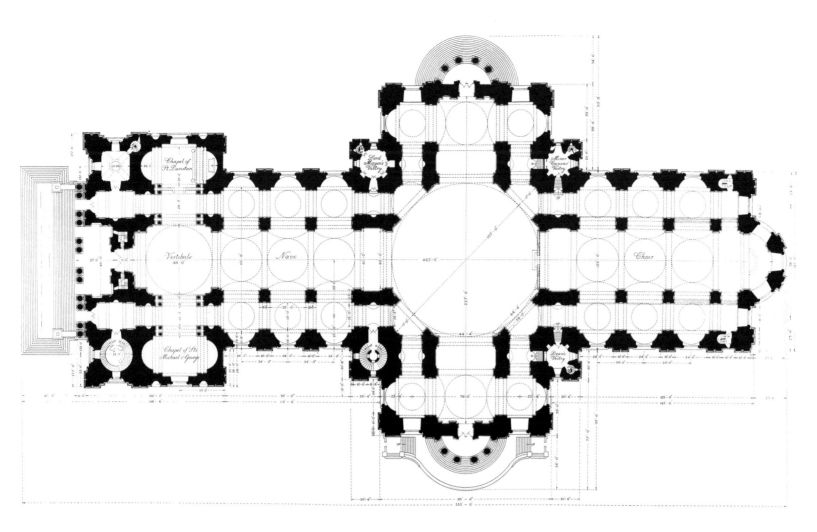

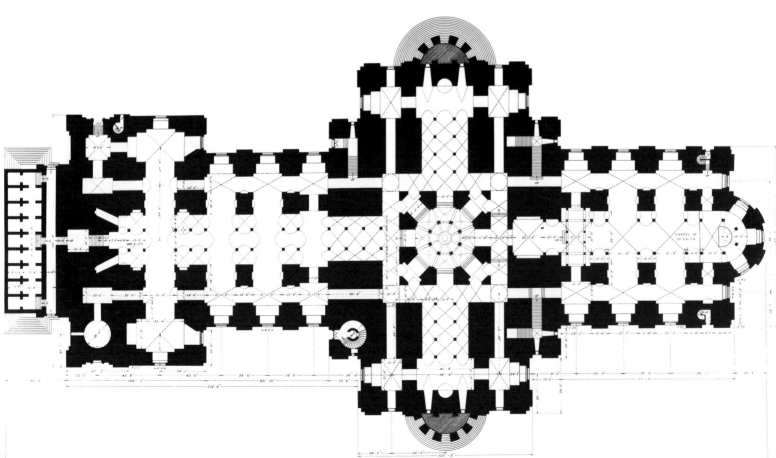

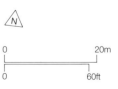

0   20m

0   60ft

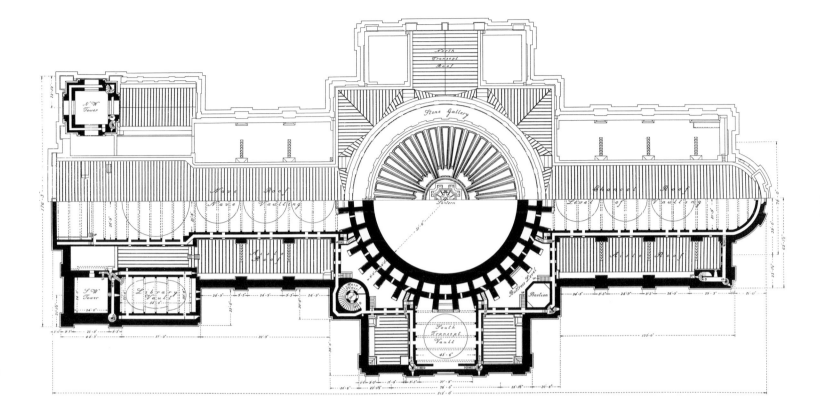

Drawings

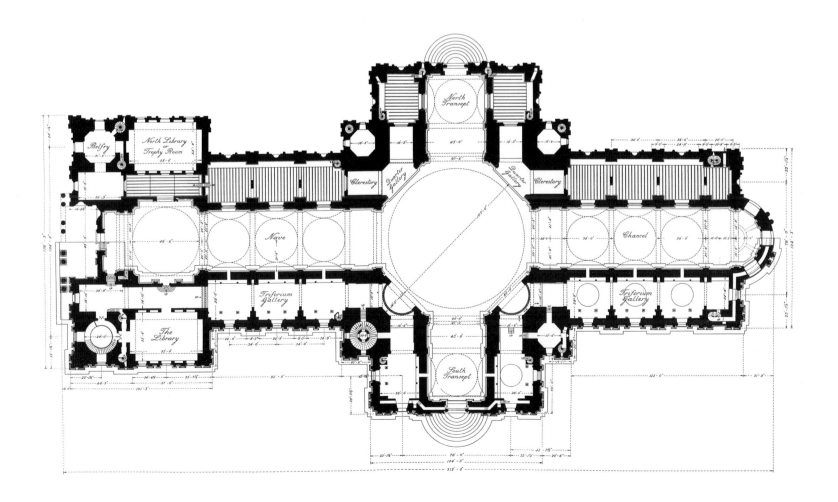

The measured drawings used here were produced by Arthur Poley (d 1956) and published by him in *St Paul's Cathedral, London, Measured, Drawn and Described*, London, 1927. These drawings were the first to record accurately the dimensions of Wren's Cathedral. Having started in 1908 with the intention of measuring the pediment of the west portico, Poley was given the opportunity by successive repair and restoration works over the following 20 years to make a detailed survey of the whole fabric of the Cathedral. In 1920 he was rewarded with the RIBA Silver Medal for his measured drawing of the west front of St Paul's.

Elevation of south front

0   15m

0   45ft

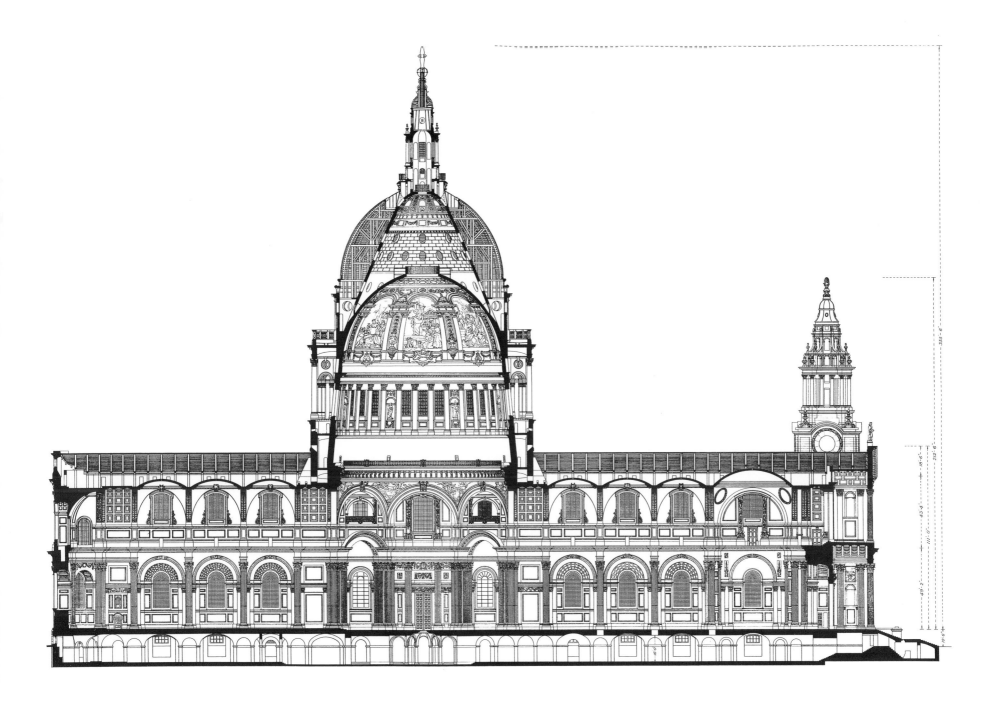

Clock tower

Left to right:

Elevation

Plans at A, B, C, D

Half diagonal section

Half normal section

Plan of roof structure

0   3m

0   10ft

Lower portion of bell tower

179' - 0"

92' - 6"

11' - 0"

0   5m

0   15ft

0   2m

0   5ft

Elevation and section of
west portico pediment

6'-0"   13'-0"   6'-0"   15'-0"

0   2m

0   5ft

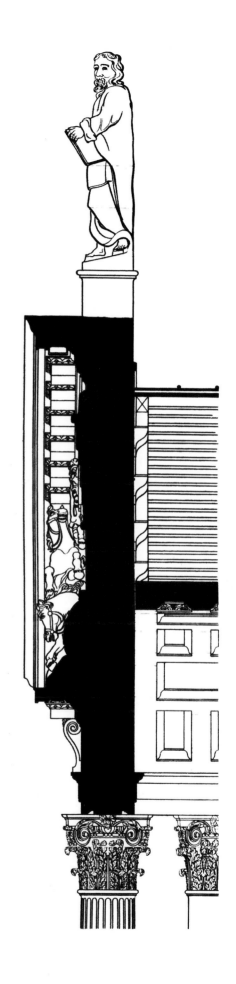

6'-0"

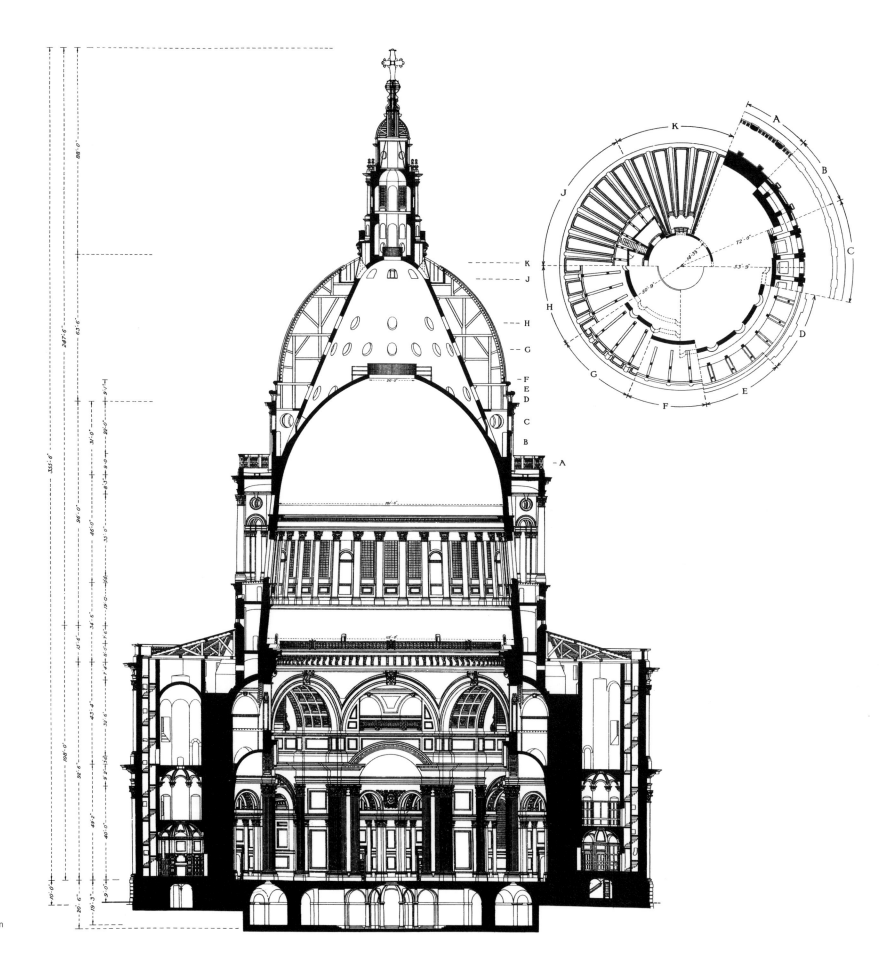

Plans through crossing

A Roof
B Peristyle
C Buttress level
D Quarter gallery
E Vaulting
F Triforium gallery
G Ground floor
H Crypt

A   B

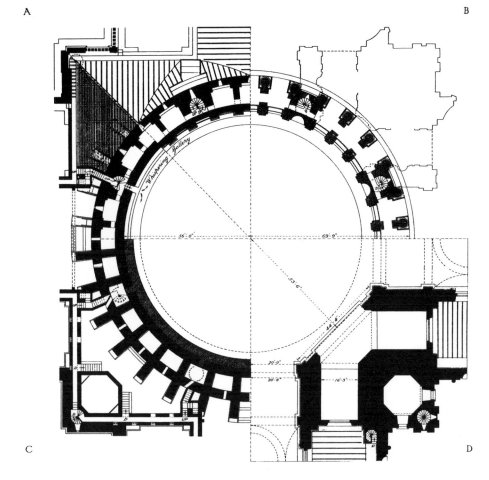

C   D

E   F

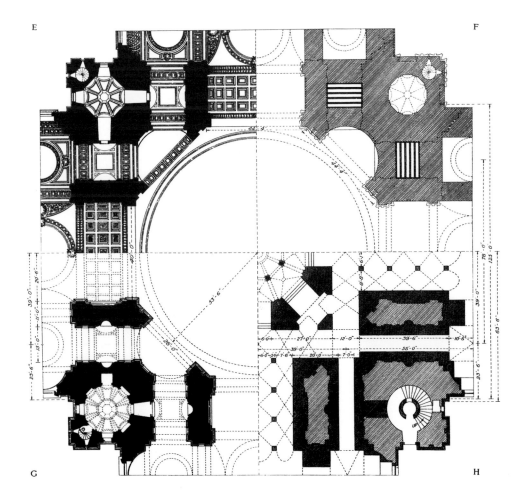

0   10m

0   30ft

G   H

**Sections through
barrel vault**

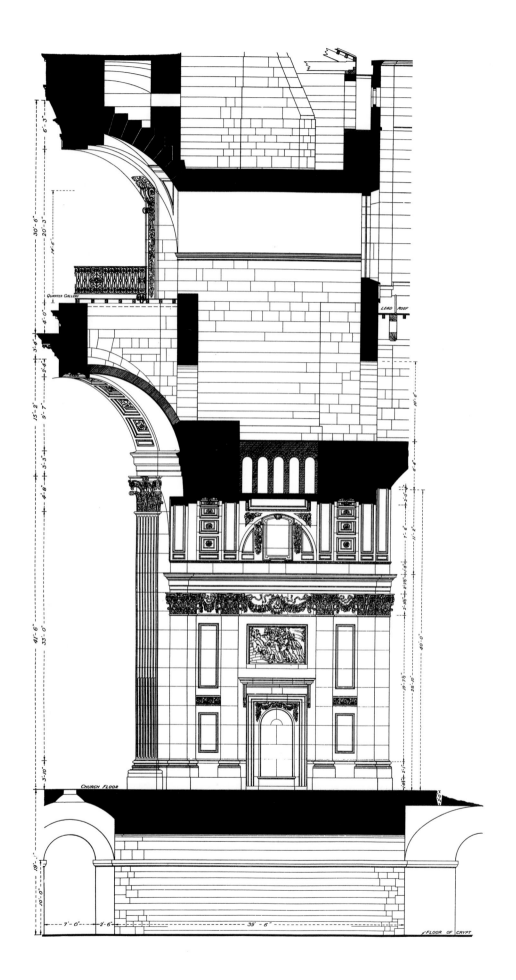

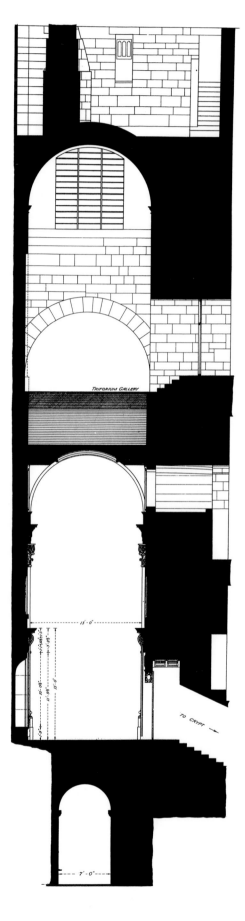

Cross section through choir

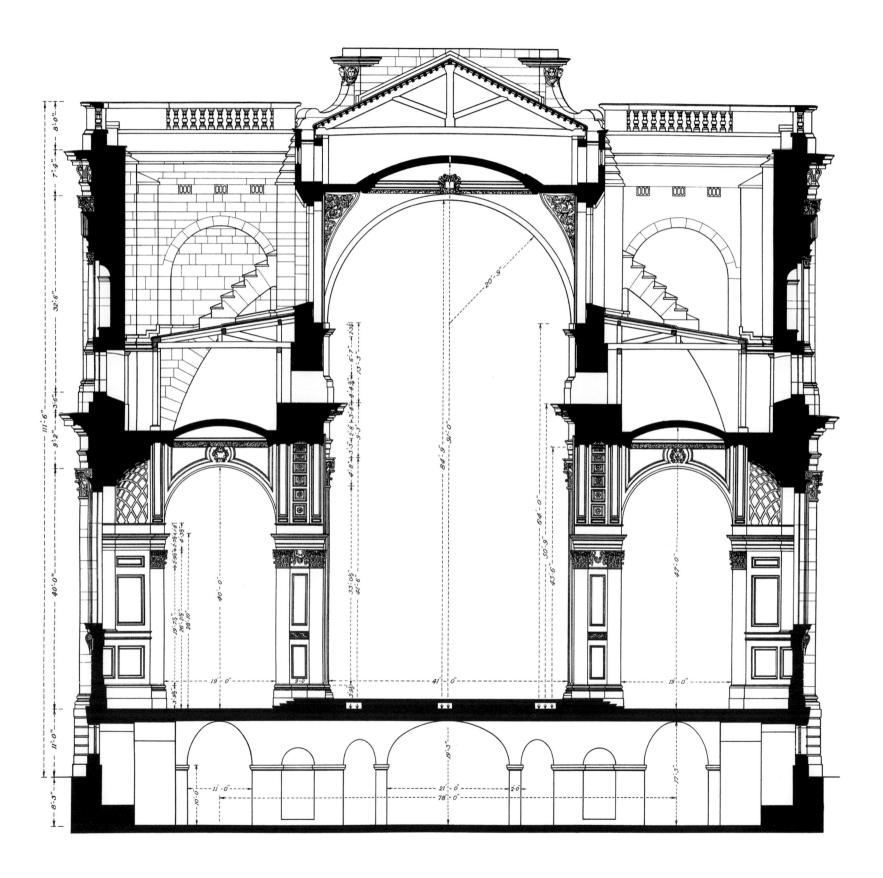

Author's acknowledgements

I should like to thank Martin Wilkinson, lecturer in lighting in the School of Architecture and Building Engineering, Bath University, England, for his calculations on the orientation of the Cathedral with respect to the sun. Dr Jennifer Nutkins provided invaluable advice on the text. The librarians at the British Library, Guildhall Library, St Paul's Cathedral Library, All Souls, Oxford, and Public Records Office should also be thanked. I am, however, particularly indebted to the librarians in the Rare Books Department of Cambridge University Library.

Publisher's acknowledgements

The publisher would like to thank the following for providing illustrations: All Soul's Library, Oxford: figs 35, 39, 46, 48–50; British Architectural Library, RIBA, London: fig 64, and drawings on p 2 and pp 46–59; Guildhall Library, London: figs 27–30, 37, 38, 41, 57, 63; Angelo Hornak: figs 9, 17, 32, 33; The President and Council of the Royal Society: fig 1.

Bibliography

Primary Sources

Campbell, C, *Vitruvius Britannicus* (London, 1715–25).
Dugdale, W, [Sir T Herbert], *The History of St Paul's Cathedral in London … Whereunto is added, a Continuation thereof, setting forth what was done in the structure of the new church, to the Year 1685* (London, 1716 ed).
Evelyn, J, *An Account of Architects and Architecture* (London, 1706).
Fréart, R, *Parallèle de l'Architecture antique et de la moderne* (Paris, 1650). Trans by Evelyn, J, *A Parallel of the Ancient Architecture with the Modern* (London, 1664).
Perrault, C, *Ordonnance des cinq espèces de colonnes selon la méthode des Anciens* (Paris, 1683). Trans by James, J, *A Treatise of the Five Orders of Columns* (London, 1708).
Pratt, R, 'St Paul's and the New Way of Architecture for Churches' (1672), in *The Architecture of Sir Roger Pratt*, ed R T Gunther (Oxford University Press, 1928).
Wren, S, *Parentalia: Or, Memoirs of the Family of the Wrens* (London, 1750). Reprinted as *Life and Works of Sir Christopher Wren from the Parentalia, or Memoirs by His Son Christopher*, ed E J Enthoven (London, 1903). Wren's Cathedral drawings (at All Souls, Oxford) and Work's Accounts (at the Guildhall Library) are published in Bolton, A T, Hendry, H P, eds, *Wren Society Publications*, 20 vols (Oxford, 1924–43): vols I–III [Cathedral drawings], V [city design], XIII–XVI, XVIII–IXX [accounts]. *Calendar of State Papers* (Domestic) 1660–1720.

Secondary Sources

Addleshaw, G, Etchells, F, *The Architectural Setting of Anglican Worship* (London: Faber and Faber, 1948).
Beard, G, *The Work of Christopher Wren* (Edinburgh: Bloomsbury, 1982).
Bennett, J A, *The Mathematical Sciences of Christopher Wren* (Cambridge University Press, 1982).
Downes, K, *The Architecture of Wren* (London: Granada, 1982).
Downes, K, *Sir Christopher Wren: The Design of St Paul's Cathedral* (London: Trefoil, 1988).
Dutton, R, *The Age of Wren* (London: Batsford, 1951).
Furst, V, *The Architecture of Sir Christopher Wren* (London: Lund Humphries, 1956).
Hart, V, *Art and Magic in the Court of the Stuarts* (London: Routledge, 1994).
Hart, V, 'London, St Paul's Architecture', *Macmillan Dictionary of Art*, (London: Macmillan, forthcoming 1995).
Hutchison, H, *Sir Christopher Wren, A Biography* (London: Victor Gollancz, 1976).
Lang, J, *Rebuilding St Paul's after the Great Fire of London* (Oxford University Press, 1956).
Mare, E, *Wren's London* (London: The Folio Society, 1975).
Rykwert, J, *The First Moderns* (Cambridge, MA and London: MIT Press, 1980).
Summerson, J, *Sir Christopher Wren* (London: Collins, 1953).
Watkin, D J, (ed), 'Architects': *Sale Catalogues of Libraries of Eminent Persons* (London: Mansell with Sotheby Parke-Bernet, 1972).
Whinney, M, *Wren* (London: Thames and Hudson, 1971).

Articles

Bennett, J A, 'Christopher Wren: Astronomy, Architecture and the Mathematical Sciences', *Journal for the History of Astronomy*, vol 6 (1975), pp 149–84.
Bennett, J A, 'Christopher Wren: The Natural Causes of Beauty', *Architectural History*, vol 15 (1972), pp 5–22.
Conder, E, 'King Charles II at the Royal Exchange, London in 1667', *Ars Quatuor Coronatorum*, vol xi (1898), pp 138–51.
Harris, E, 'Wren', in British Architectural Books and Writers 1556–1785 (Cambridge University Press, 1990), pp 503–508.
Summerson, J, 'The Mind of Wren', in *Heavenly Mansions and Other Essays on Architecture* (London: Norton, 1949), pp 51–86.
Summerson, J, 'Sir Christopher Wren, P R S (1632–1723)', *Notes and Records of the Royal Society of London*, vol 15, (1960) pp 99–105: *The Unromantic Castle* (London: Thames and Hudson, 1990), pp 63–8.
Summerson, J, 'The Penultimate Design for St Paul's', *Burlington Magazine*, vol 103 (1961), pp 83–9: *ibid* (1990), pp 69–78.

Chronology

1632 Christopher Wren born on 20 October at East Knoyle, Wiltshire, where his father was Rector.

1650 Awarded BA at Wadham College, Oxford.

1653 Appointed Fellow of All Souls College, Oxford.

1657 Appointed Professor of Astronomy, Gresham College, London.

1661 Appointed Savilian Professor of Astronomy at Oxford; founder member of the Royal Society. Wren absent from Oxford during October due to repair of Old St Paul's.

1663 18 April, the Royal Commission for repair of old St Paul's Cathedral, Wren not a member.

1663–5 Designs Pembroke College chapel, Cambridge.

1664–9 Designs Sheldonian Theatre, Oxford.

1665 Departs for Paris in June, and escapes the plague.

1666 Returns to London in early March. 'Pre-fire' project for Old St Paul's: 7 May report to Dean on new crossing, 5 August drawings for crossing, 27 August site meeting. Following the 'Great Fire' of London (2 September) appointed member of the Royal Commission for rebuilding the capital, and prepares plan.

1668 Report on Salisbury Cathedral; 25 April Dean requests re-submission of earlier drawings of scheme for St Paul's, 25 July order for demolition of tower and choir of Old St Paul's.

1668–73 Designs Emmanuel College chapel, Cambridge.

1669 Appointed Surveyor-General of the King's Works; marries Faith Coghill.

1669–74 Designs the Customs House, London.

1670 March, First Model of scheme for St Paul's completed.

1670–1 Designs St Dunstan-in-the-East.

1670–3 Designs St Vedast, Foster Lane.

1670–6 Designs St Mary at Hill, Thames Street.

1670–9 Designs St Edmund King and Martyr.

1670–80 Designs St Mary-le-Bow, Cheapside.

1670–84 Designs St Bride, Fleet Street.

1671–6 Designs St Magnus Martyr, Lower Thames Street. Designs the Monument.

1671–7 Designs St Lawrence, Jewry. Designs St Nicholas, Cole Abbey.

1672 Before 25 March, Wren paid £100 for Greek cross scheme drawings for St Paul's.

1672–9 Designs St Stephen, Walbrook.

1673 Wren knighted. The Great Model of Wren's Greek cross scheme for St Paul's built; 12 July Sir Roger Pratt's criticism of the First Model. Summer, scaffolding and standard to set out centre of dome. 22 September, Wren and Woodroffe scale up drawings of Great Model for joiner. 12 November, Warrant for establishing rebuilding commission, Great Model approved.

1674 8 August, Hooke saw Great Model finished.

1675 14 May Warrant for revised, Latin cross scheme for St Paul's – 'Warrant Design' – 15 July first foundation contracts confirmed, 17 August contracts confirmed for above-ground masonry. Designs the Royal Observatory, Greenwich; birth of a son, Christopher.

1676 November, St Paul's transept foundations begun.

1676–83 Designs St James, Garlickhythe.

1676–84 Trinity College library, Cambridge.

1677 Second marriage, to Jane Fitzwilliam.

1677–80 Designs St Anne and St Agnes, Gresham Street.

1677–83 Designs St Benet, Paul's Wharf and St Mildred, Bread Street.

1677–84 Designs St Martin, Ludgate.

1677–85 Designs St Swithin, Cannon Street.

1677–87 Designs Christ Church, Newgate Street.

1678 September St Paul's nave foundations begun.

1678–82 Designs St Antholin, Watling Street (demolished 1873).

1680–2 Designs St Clement Danes.

1680–6 Designs St Anne, Soho.

1681–2 Designs Tom Tower, Christ Church, Oxford.

1681–3 Appointed President of the Royal Society.

1681–6 Designs St Mary Abchurch.

1682–4 Designs St James', Piccadilly.

1682–91 Designs Royal Hospital at Chelsea.

1683–5 Designs Winchester Palace.

1685 Choir and transept walls at St Paul's reach the top of the lower Order.

1685–7 Designs chapel and Privy Gallery, Whitehall Palace.

1686–94 Designs St Michael, Paternoster Royal.

1689–1701 Designs Hampton Court and Kensington Palaces.

1691–3 The Queen's Apartments, Whitehall Palace.

1694 Commencement of fittings in choir of St Paul's.

1696–1702 Designs Greenwich Hospital.

1697 2 December first service in the choir of St Paul's.

1698 Prepares schemes for rebuilding at Whitehall Palace after fire. St Paul's dome reaches Whispering Gallery level.

1698–1722 Repairs to Westminster Abbey.

1699 Carving by Caius Gabriel Cibber of a sunburst framing a phoenix in southern transept pediment.

1704 February final design for towers of St Paul's.

1706 Portico of St Paul's completed.

1707 Brick cone of dome of St Paul's built.

1708 Outer dome leaded at St Paul's; lantern masonry.

1709–11 Designs Marlborough House, St James'.

1710 Wren's last official attendance at the commission for St Paul's.

1711 St Paul's declared finished.

1718 Wren deprived of the title of Surveyor General.

1723 Wren dies in London.

1750 *Parentalia* (compiled by son) is published by Wren's grandson, Stephen.

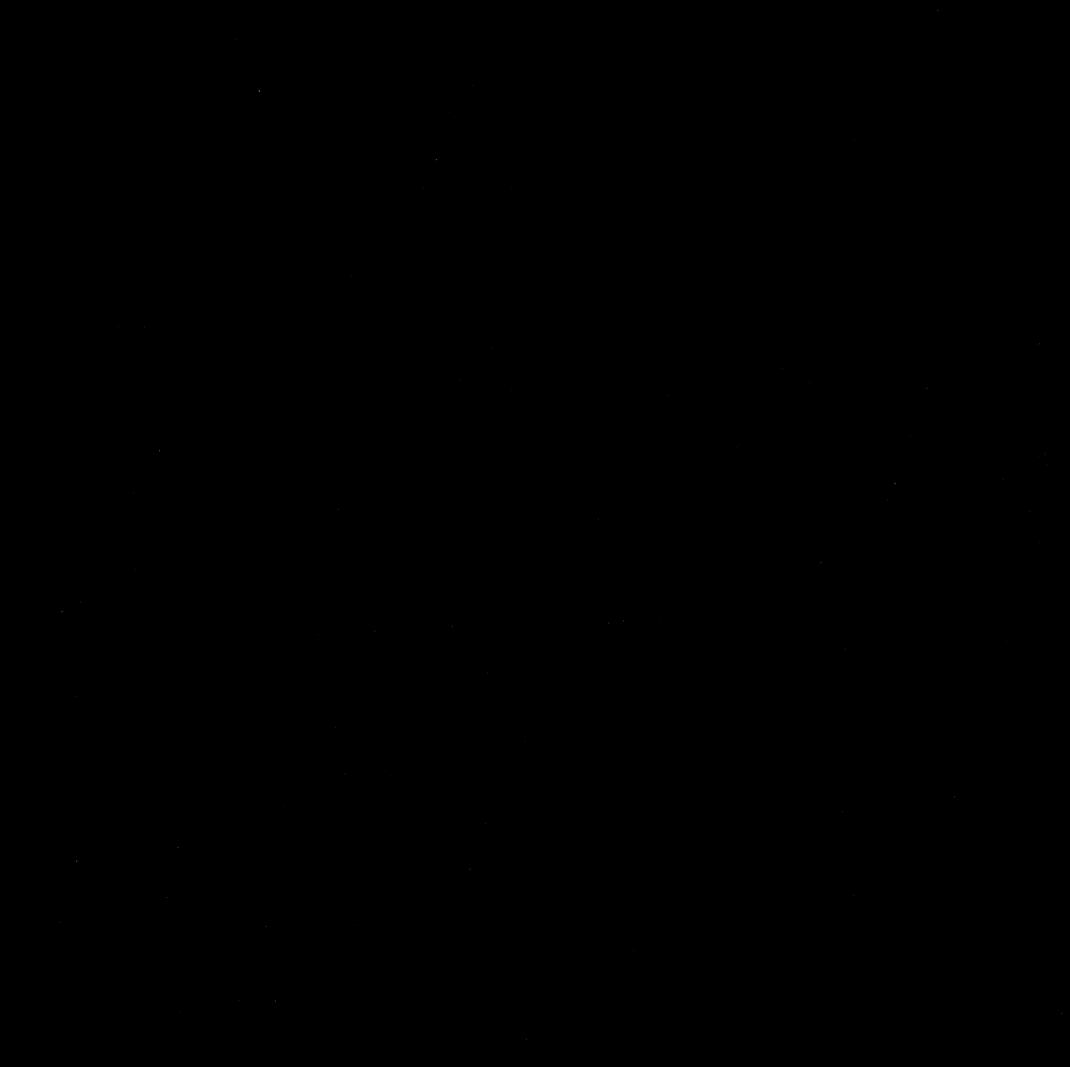

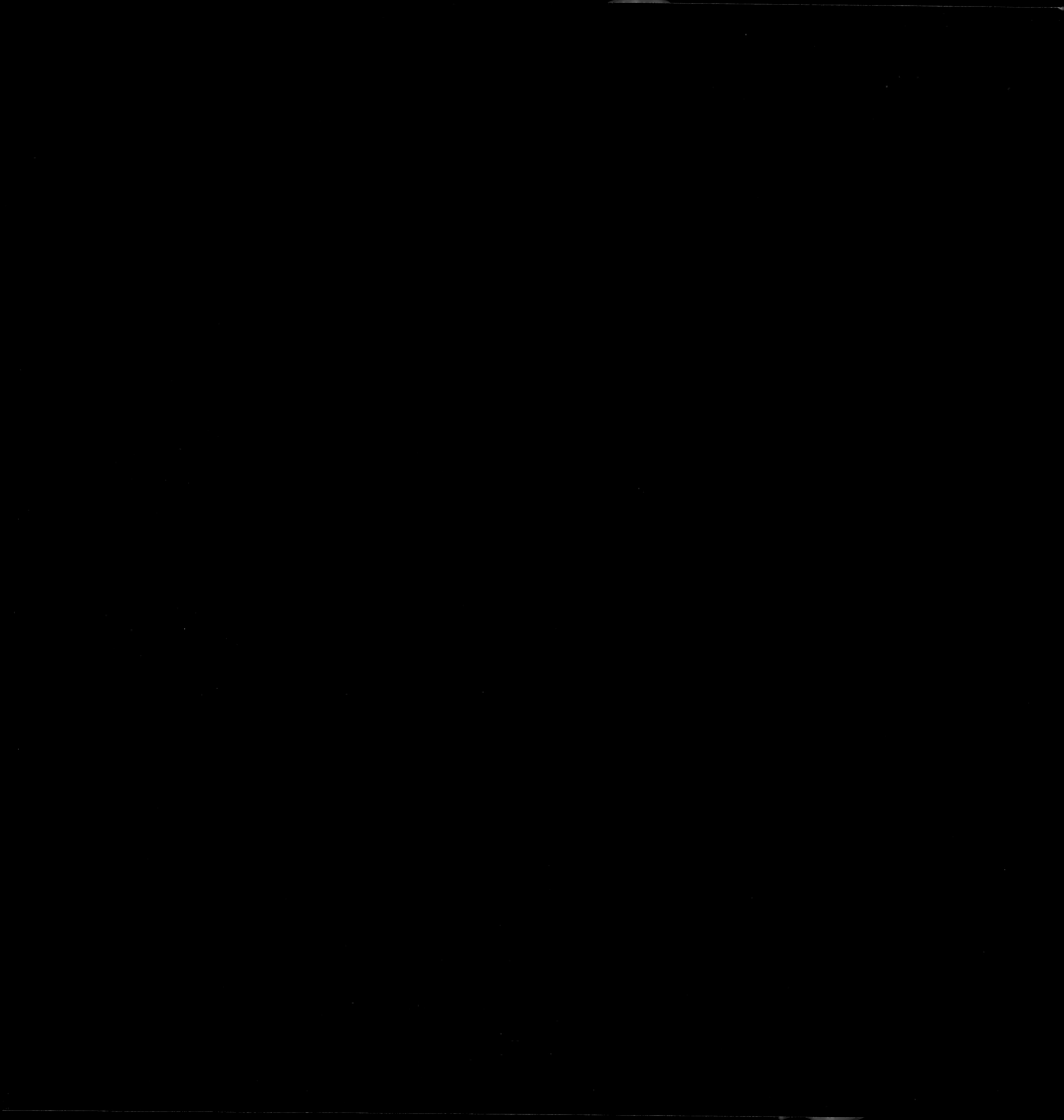

Jože Plečnik
Church of the Sacred Heart
Prague 1922–33

Ivan Margolius

Photography
Mark Fiennes; cover detail
also by Mark Fiennes
Drawings
John Hewitt

1 Jože Plečnik in 1916.
2 The Church of the Sacred
Heart from the southeast.

In front of each of Plečnik's works we say
to ourselves: What a unique proposal!
What an unusual, individual idea! What an
original approach to massing! And, at the
same time, how we sense the human spirit!
Pavel Janák, *Volné směry*, 1927

1

Plečnik in Prague

The Church of the Sacred Heart proudly
dominates a quiet green square of the
Vinohrady quarter and, with its majestic
presence, securely anchors the borough
into Prague's panorama. This is an
intriguing building and its unique
appearance and monumental quality
attracts every passer-by. The dark brown
brickwork punctuated with grey granite
stones contains an unusual masterpiece,
judged by many as one of the best
architectural creations of Slovenian
architect, Jože Plečnik.

Jože Plečnik was born in Ljubljana,
Slovenia in 1872 and came to Prague to
teach and work in 1911. Plečnik studied
architecture at Otto Wagner's studio in the
Viennese Fine Arts Academy from 1895.
One of his fellow students was Jan Kotěra,
who later became a founder of the Czech
Modern Movement. Their friendship
and bond increased with the closer
understanding and acknowledgement of
their Slavonic background. Both were very
talented students and received the *Prix de
Rome* scholarship, Kotěra a year before
Plečnik. This award enabled them to travel
through Europe, Plečnik spending most of
his time in Italy and France and thoroughly
immersing himself in Roman, Gothic and
Renaissance architecture.

On completion of his studies Plečnik
started working for Otto Wagner and later
set up his own office in Vienna. Kotěra, in
the meantime, returned to Prague but they
kept in touch, informing each other
about their careers in architecture. Plečnik
built several small houses, villas and
monuments in the Austrian capital and
by 1902 Kotěra was able to write an article
in the Prague magazine *Volné směry* (*Free
Tendencies*) about Plečnik and his work:

Plečnik is a man who has a fixed goal and
who advances towards it with a will of iron,
conscious of each step he takes and
subjecting his progression to unwavering
self-criticism. He does not allow himself to
be stopped by disappointment, or even –
and this is more uncommon still – by worldly
success… He understood and absorbed the
spirit of antiquity while travelling in Italy. He
loves folklore art and finds there simplicity
and bitterness. Sometimes it is bitterness
in its basic sense, sometimes soft lyricism in
a modest formal arrangement…[1]

In 1903 Plečnik was commissioned to
design a large building in the centre of
Vienna, later called Zacherl after the client.
The Zacherl House was completed to
mixed reception in 1905. Plečnik was
already establishing certain architectural
elements which he later reused in Prague –
the simple granite facade, exquisitely
detailed, suddenly stopping below the last,
top level with another building appearing
to rise out of the stone base, richly
embellished with Secessionist motifs.
Other successful projects continued
including the Church of the Holy Spirit in
Ottakring where Plečnik pioneered the use
of reinforced concrete in an artistic rather
than utilitarian way.

2

3

4

5

3 Plečnik's Zacherl House, Vienna, 1903–05, the upper part of the facade.
4, 5 Plečnik's Chapel of St John, Žale Cemetery, Ljubljana, 1938–40 is intriguing when compared with René Magritte's painting *La Voix du silence*, 1928.

Plečnik's continued stay in Vienna was partly motivated by his possible succession to Wagner's position at the Fine Arts Academy. However, Plečnik was not chosen by the government officials despite having the support of the Academy students. His Slavonic background in the days of rising Austrian nationalism certainly did not help.

In this difficult time, when even in his native Slovenia Plečnik was not understood and welcomed, Kotěra, who vacated his teaching position at the Prague Institute of Decorative Arts to found an architectural studio at the Prague Fine Arts Academy, offered Plečnik his previous post. Plečnik accepted confirming to Kotěra: 'I put my fate in your hands…'.[2] Thus, early in 1911, Prague's architectural education arena held two important personalities who were both taught by Otto Wagner. For ten years Plečnik devoted most of his time to teaching, occasionally making trips to Vienna to oversee the completion of his building projects. After the beginning of the First World War he exclusively taught architecture at the Institute and during that time did not produce any significant realized work.

Plečnik's design attitudes

Plečnik was a deeply religious man with high Slavonic convictions and a love of his Slovenian homeland. These attitudes were inevitably impressed on his work, which stood apart from projects executed by his contemporaries. Plečnik's aim was to reinforce the art content in his architecture. The architectural compositions were conceived in a singular and startling way to force the building's user, visitor and spectator to reflect actively on and interact with Plečnik's creations.

Plečnik's work was full of symbolism, religious feeling and reverence for the pure elements of architecture. It was also full of contrasts and contradictions, but at the same time was gracefully conceived and constructed. As, for example, was the expression of positive and negative, present and future, and life and death, underlined in Plečnik's Chapel of St John in Žale Cemetery, Ljubljana (1938–40) with its dark, mysterious entrance on the left and bright wall with a window and an amphora jar on the right separated by a central column. Plečnik echoed feelings evoked by the Belgian artist René Magritte when he created his Surrealist painting, *La Voix du silence* (1928), showing dark, unknown space on the left separated, by a partition, from a room interior on the right.

6

7

Architect Otakar Novotný in his biography of Jan Kotěra, published in 1958, succinctly summarized Plečnik's comprehensive approach to design:

Plečnik derives his work from classical antiquity but he also worships other historical styles and studies their forms; only he submits them to logical analysis and reshapes them into a picture of modernity. They are not really very new forms but they are such as they have never been before and which could only be thought out by him. Not in the comfort of his studio, but in intimate contact with the material from which he captures form. Not wholly functional, but not that non-functional; with the strength of his feelings and intellect, with material which, in his hands, lives many times, primitively and craftily, but always artistically…[3]

The three schemes

The site for the Church of the Sacred Heart is situated within the Prague settlement of Viničné Hory or Vinohrady (Vineyard Hills) which was founded in an area stretching from Wenceslas Square, previously the Horse Market, uphill and eastwards out of the city. In the fourteenth century, vineyards attached to large farmsteads were laid out there. From these beginnings, beyond the original city walls, a suburb developed. In 1867, when Bohemia was part of the large Austro-Hungarian Empire, this section of Prague gained the Emperor Franz Joseph's assent to be called Královské (Royal) Vinohrady. In 1879 Vinohrady was the first Prague suburb to be elevated to town status. At that time its 15,000 inhabitants could only worship in school chapels. When the population increased to over 34,500 in 1890, it was decided that Vinohrady needed its own church. The first Catholic church, dedicated to St Ludmila, was erected at Náměstí Míru (Peace Square) and designed in a neo-Gothic style by Josef Mocker. The church was consecrated in 1893.

8

9

6, 7 Wenceslas Square in Prague: a half-mile long, broad avenue boarded by hotels, banks, shops and offices.
8, 9 The city of Prague is well known for the number and variety of its churches and towers which terminate vistas created by the narrow streets.
10 The Cathedral of St Vitus, surrounded by Prague Castle, crowns Hradčany Hill rising above the River Vltava.
11 View from Prague Castle onto the city.

10

11

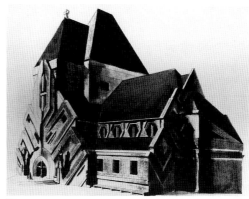

14

With the beginning of the new century the Vinohrady population grew to 50,000, of which 90 per cent was of Catholic persuasion. In 1908 the town gave the newly established second Catholic church administration a site within the Jiří z Poděbrad Square (Jiří z Poděbrad being a Czech king between 1458 and 1471) to build another church in the borough. There followed a number of disputes about the site, which was originally given to the town by the Zdekaur family. The main city council, for example, required the square to remain in use wholly as a park. Even Czechoslovak President Masaryk was involved in discussions with the authorities. The arguments were finally resolved in May 1928, after a judgment given by the Law Faculty of the Charles University, and a site area of 91.5 metres by 32 metres within the square was confirmed.

In 1910 the town gave the church administration office premises on the square and, until the church was built, the use of a nearby school chapel consecrated to St Alois. Most importantly, an Association for the Construction of the Second Catholic Church at Královské Vinohrady was founded in March 1914 led by Father Hoffmann and later Father Škarda.

Finances then had to be raised for the project. It was a difficult task for the Association to resolve but had to be accomplished since the Archbishop's permission to proceed with the building could not be granted without secure resources. Various actions were taken, including collections and lotteries, and gifts were received, including an endowment by Karel Bepta of substantial plots of land in the borough. The First World War interrupted the work of the Association and renewed efforts were not made until the end of the hostilities. Furthermore, the Austro-Hungarian Empire collapsed and Prague became capital of the new Czechoslovak Republic on 28 October 1918.

Initially the Association approached Plečnik to persuade him to take on the task of designing the new church. After consideration Plečnik refused pointing out that he 'did not know sufficiently the religious soul of the people of Prague'.[4]

Father Škarda decided to discuss the church project with a Prague architect, Antonín Mikeš, who proposed a neo-Romanesque basilica design. However, nothing came of this proposal and, in 1919, with the help of architects Bureš, Kotěra and Hilbert, the Association set up an anonymous architectural competition for the new second Catholic church for Vinohrady. The prizes were set at 8,000, 6,000 and 4,000 Czech crowns. The competition conditions asked for the church design to reflect the remembrance of the newly established Czechoslovak Republic. Consideration of the suitable setting of the church within the square and the use of the residual space was also required. The jury consisted of Bishop Podlaha, Father Škarda, Chaplain Tilt, town mayor Beneš and architects Kamil Hilbert, Jan Kotěra, Theodor Petřík, Dr Beneš and Josef Fanta.

In October 1919 the results were announced. 31 designs were submitted, mostly from young architects. The majority of the proposals were of a traditional, classical character, but with two notable exceptions. One was Jiří Kroha's suggestion of a church in the Cubist style. This architectural trend was established in Bohemia before the First World War as a direct reaction to the Cubist paintings of Picasso, Braque and Gris. The other was Josef Kalous' Modernist proposal. However, the competition jury chose three non-controversial schemes. The winning design, entitled *19 M 19,* was from Jindřich Merganc and the runners-up were the two

12

13

15 **16**

projects *Alfa Omega* from Alois Mezera and *Three Circles K V* from the architects Leden and Vacek. Yet none of these designs were actually adopted, the reason being a letter sent to Plečnik on 4 April 1919 during the competition from the Association of Czech Architects of which Plečnik was a founder member:

Honoured Professor,
Having deliberated over the competition currently being prepared for the construction of a second Catholic church in Vinohrady, our Association has arrived at the conviction that this competition could produce nothing better and more authentic than a work created by you. We have long been hoping that Prague would one day be enriched with a work of your hands, a work that we are certain would constitute one of its greatest jewels. Consequently, we suggested to the association organizing the competition that the competition be cancelled and that we entrust the work directly to you. We are now informed that it is too late to cancel the public competition, but the jury suggests that we ask you to submit a project *hors-concours*. We are therefore unanimously requesting that you undertake this task under these conditions. We assure you that we are asking this out of common accord, in all sincerity, and with the hope that you will not refuse.[5]

This letter was signed by 29 architects including well known personalities such as Josef Gočár, Pavel Janák, Josef Chochol, Vlastislav Hofman, Otakar Novotný and Oldřich Tyl. Both Jindřich Merganc and Alois Mezera, Plečnik students, were among the signatories. This generous act was a way of rewarding Plečnik for his long devoted teaching period at the Institute of Decorative Arts.

Soon after this offer Plečnik was further recognized by being introduced to President Masaryk by Kotěra and was subsequently commissioned to carry out restoration work at Prague Castle, including the remodelling of the Castle gardens. This activity kept Plečnik

occupied for the next 15 years. Also at this time, in 1920, Plečnik was offered a professorship of architecture at the newly established University of Ljubljana, and in April 1921 he left Prague to return permanently to Slovenia. Nevertheless, due to the amount of work in Prague, Plečnik travelled there during university holidays to attend to his continued work on site. He appointed Otto Rothmayer, one of his more gifted students, to supervise projects in his absence.

15 Plečnik's restoration work at Prague Castle: Paradise Garden steps leading up to the Garden entrance gate, 1920–27.
16 The shallow granite steps of the Paradise Garden adjoin the ancient brick castle walls, contrasting in material and form.
17 Plečnik's Měřín granite table, shaded by a timber pergola supported on stone columns, at the Moravian Bastion, Ramparts Garden at Prague Castle, 1923.
18 Plečnik's horizontal granite beam beside the Slavata Monument, Ramparts Garden, 1920–27.

17

18

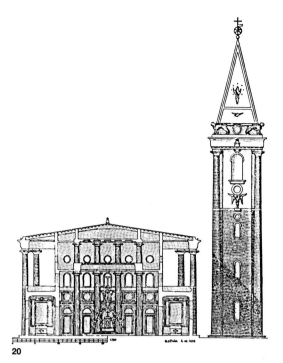

20

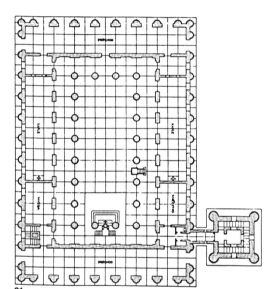

21

The letter from the Czech architects encouraged the Association for the Second Catholic Church to persuade Plečnik to submit his proposal. Initially, in 1921, because of difficulties with the site, Plečnik proposed to extend the St Alois chapel with a large rotunda design wedged between the apartment buildings and entered from the existing chapel on the north side of the square. However, this idea was not acceptable to the Association; thus, in December 1922 Plečnik sent his first scheme of a new church standing within the square, giving this work to the church commission free of charge as he similarly submitted all the following designs.

Plečnik's proposals were viewed against the rise of Purist and Functionalist architecture which began to emerge in Czechoslovakia after 1922 as a consequence of the Cubist era and general world design developments in the USA, France, Germany and Holland. It should be noted that Plečnik's designs, especially his later schemes, were met with apprehension and misunderstanding by the contemporary Prague architectural community. They were seen to be conceived in a traditional, classical manner against the prevailing trend. Plečnik's proposals, however, were so advanced that they could only be fully appreciated after a substantial period of time, when the public's mind had broadened enough to understand Plečnik's intentions and ideas. It is also interesting to note how each scheme he proposed was radically different both in planning and architectural terms.

The first scheme was based on a Greek temple but of Schinkelesque proportions and influence. It was a large monumental building with columns on all sides containing another structure within, which reduced in size on the upper level. A tall Italian bell tower, or campanile, with a steep pitched roof stood by the northeast corner connected to the temple by a modest corridor. The central nave was defined by a line of internal columns which separated narrow side aisles containing enclosed chapels. A timber model of this scheme still exists and is now stored in the church.

22

23

An alternative based on the same plan but with a different facade treatment was also produced in 1922. The overall form of the temple was retained but the columns were replaced by a solid wall enclosure punched with small semicircular arched windows at ground level and larger ones at first-floor level revealing the secondary building held within. Both of these schemes, however, were too expensive for the Church Association and Plečnik was asked to resubmit a cheaper version.

While working on the Prague church Plečnik was approached by Franciscan priests in Ljubljana who requested a new Church of St Francis of Assisi at Šiška. Inevitably this church, with a tall east classical tower and unusual central altar, built between 1925 and 1931, influenced the designs for the Sacred Heart.

The second scheme sent to the Association in 1925 concentrated on a new interior concept. The main space consisted of one large spatial nave without additional aisles, but surrounded by a narrow corridor. The nave was organized by the rigid placing of five main structural columns, one in the centre representing Jesus Christ and four columns placed towards each corner embodying His Evangelists.

24

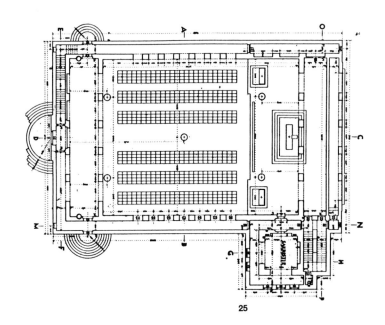

25

23–25 West and south elevations and plan of the second scheme, 1925.
26 Church of St Francis of Assisi, Šiška, Ljubljana, 1925–31. Here, Plečnik used tall narrow pyramids to strengthen the base of the bell tower.

26

30

27 Stone pyramid in the Ramparts Garden, Prague Castle, is used to reinforce the axis of the view from Plečnik's Bull Staircase onto the Baroque church of St Nicholas at Malá Strana.
28 The central column of Plečnik's entrance gate to the Paradise Garden, Prague Castle.
29 Plečnik's Belvedere Pavilion, Ramparts Garden, 1920–27.
30 A typical Plečnik feature: a column on the centre line of an opening or element; here shown at the Plečnik Hall, Prague Castle, 1928–30.

27

28

29

The nave was lit by a line of clerestory windows. The tower, now a more massive feature, was attached to the main building but this time in the southeast corner. Externally the whole building was decorated with circular motifs and large, overlapping semicircular arched windows, Plečnik's preferred architectural tools. On top of the cornice and the tower were decorative pillars. But, again, this scheme did not meet the Association's budget and thus Plečnik was requested to rework his proposals.

The symbol of the central column clearly shown in the second option was a typical feature of Plečnik's work. It is found in many of his projects from the 1920s onwards, particularly in his work at Prague Castle and later in Ljubljana. The central column represented the mystical in Plečnik: his conception of a human being as the centre of the universe, his elevation of the strength of the human spirit above all else, and the notion that religious belief is the pivotal point of life. The concept of placing a strong element on the centre line of an architectural composition, in the line of natural vision, was surprising and against established architectural rules. It was Plečnik's statement against functionalist ideology and he persistently employed this arrangement to startling effect. As such, his signature is left by the column in front of the circular opening in the Plečnik Hall at Prague Castle, by the supporting columns on the centre line of the stairway leading from the third Castle courtyard to the Ramparts Garden, by the slender pyramid reinforcing the line of vision to the Church of St Nicholas, and by the central column at the gate entrance to the Paradise Garden.

The third set of drawings came close to the final scheme as realized. This proposal, received by the Association in 1927, showed another totally different scheme but of much better quality and originality than the previous designs. The main differences to the built scheme was the omission of four large, circular brick columns placed at the corners of the main tower. These were replaced by two tall, slender pyramids, one on either side of the tower. Also, the large glazed clock faces were simplified, the door portals were rendered rather than laid in ashlar, and the row of angels in relief below the top cornice was substituted by a line of Roman-derived simple, suspended, cloth-like garland motifs. The crypt was originally of rectangular section and the side altars were irregularly arranged in the nave. Most of these changes were made for financial reasons, keeping the building budget to a minimum.

31

32

31, 32, 34 The west, east and south elevations of the third scheme for the Church of the Sacred Heart showing brick cylindrical columns either side of the clock tower, 1927.

33 Plan of the nave floor with the altar disposition as originally proposed, 1927.

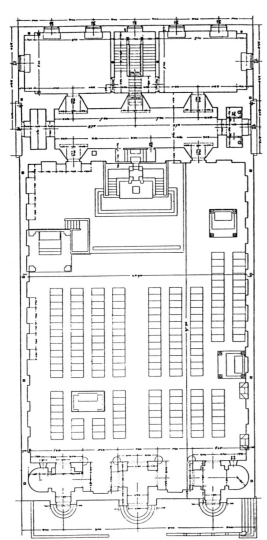

33

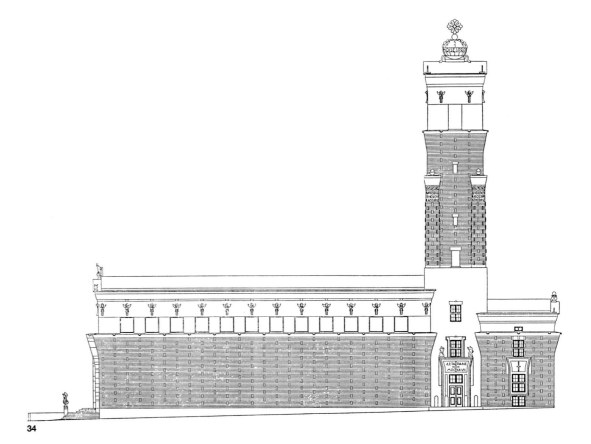

34

35

36

The Vinohrady church

One of the main problems with the project that Plečnik had to resolve was how to place the new church in the large park of Jiří z Poděbrad Square. Most of the architects who took part in the 1919 competition struggled to achieve a well-balanced layout. The church was almost always placed in the eastern, upper part of the square and the rest filled with small subsidiary buildings or enclosures defined by colonnades in front of the church. This way the size of the square was reduced and a more comfortable setting achieved. However, the lack of finances governed Plečnik's own modest, final solution.

Plečnik used the axes of existing streets as constructing lines to place the new building in the overflowing space of the square. The pleasant vistas from the surrounding streets framed by buildings on either side justified this concept. Mánesova Street lent the main axis to the church, and Laubova and Blodkova terminating at Škroupovo Square located the position of the broad church tower. Plečnik often made use of 'lay lines' to reinforce his design concepts. The architectural elements at Prague Castle for example were endlessly interconnected from one to the other, leading the spectator along a well-defined path of discovery. The architectural features were thus located in one and only place with no alternative possible, as if derived by nature itself.

The church, as finally built, consists of three main elements. The first is a large spacious nave 37.9 metres long, 25.9 metres wide and 13 metres high. There are no additional aisles or separate chapels. There is a central altar on the east wall dedicated to the Sacred Heart, two unusual corner altars to the Virgin Mary and St Joseph and two side altars to St Antony and St Theresa. The steel roof structure concealed above the dark, polished timber, square-coffered ceiling spans across the nave. The main supporting walls are internally faced with smooth, red brickwork formed into regular pilasters and decorated with gold-plated crosses.

37

38

39

40

41

Light floods into the main, cool prayer hall from 32 clerestory windows, 24 with stained glass designs by Karel Svolinský. The stained glass designs centre on the Sacred Heart on the cross with peacocks and fish, and wheat and grape motifs. A further six plain glazed windows above the main altar filter light into the first-floor level of the tower. The windows are placed in a white-rendered band and sit on a white-rendered elevated walkway surrounding the whole nave at high level, enabling easy access to windows for cleaning. The light band of the walkway, wall and windows visually separates the dark ceiling from the brickwork below. The choir gallery above the main entrance contains the organ. The light-coloured terrazzo floor with regular, circular dark grey and red patterns, possibly inspired by textile motifs, includes small square marble inserts.

The heavy timber doors to the sacristy show tree motifs in the main panels with handles designed in the form of a bird. Above the doors are carved stone lintels with small variations for single and double openings. The main altar statues were completed by sculptors Damian Pešan and A Berka.

The second element of the church is the massive, 42-metre high clock and bell tower, its full height being the same as the overall length of the nave; but it is only six and a half metres deep. The design concept of the tower is unusual but very effective. The large glass clock faces give the tower its distinguishing look and lighten the composition which would have been very cumbersome otherwise. Two slender pyramids on the north and south side of the tower balance the design. An additional four small pyramids were planned by Plečnik, two on either side of each tall pyramid, but these were never built. The tower by its size, monumentality and location locks the church into Prague's urban landscape. To look for a parallel to the Plečnik church tower one might consider a French Gothic cathedral such as Reims with its large, wide, west tower and rose window.

42

40 Church of the Sacred Heart, access walkway along the clerestory windows.

41 The centrepiece of the altar: the tabernacle with the Sacred Heart statue above.

42–44 Carved timber doors from the nave to the sacristy and detail of a palm tree motif. The door handle is in the form of a bird, designed by Plečnik and cast by Karel Pešan. Both motifs were inspired by ancient Egyptian symbolism.

43

44

45

46

45 Concrete walkway leading up the church's tower.

46 Walkway detailing at the glazed clock dials ensures minimum visual obstruction.

47 Hollow artificial stone cylinders forming a vision and ventilation grille to the crypt.

48 Typical Plečnik freestanding balustrade panel to the staircase by the rear entrance.

49 The crypt's surface materials create a calm, spiritual atmosphere.

50 Detail of the crypt light slots, terminating in the nave floor above and glazed with translucent glass.

47

48

The interior design of the tower is markedly different to the exterior. Here Plečnik enclosed a modern, avant-garde concept of white, clean, dynamic space with a classical, heavy outside skin. To reach the clock and the six bells Plečnik designed a daring reinforced-concrete ramp which ascends like a tightly stretched ribbon. At the clock faces, the concrete balustrade upstand which also strengthens the structure is omitted to provide maximum transparency and substituted with a metal railing, with the result that the one-metre wide ramp spans an incredible nine metres without any visible means of support. The enormous clock dials of 7.6 metre diameter are simply glazed into a square grid of painted metal framework; these transparent dials were aptly described to represent both spatial and time dimensions.[6] One electric clock mechanism, connected across the width of the tower, drives the hands on both dials.

The third element of the church includes the sacristy and baptism hall at the eastern end on the ground floor. In between these rooms is the rear entrance and a staircase which leads up to the clock tower ramp at first-floor level and down to the crypt in the basement. Further rooms above the sacristy and the hall, including cellar spaces below, provide useful additional areas for the church commission.

The crypt, designed in a tunnel-like, continuous semicircular red-brick arch, has light slots carved into it at regular intervals on both sides. These slots, framed by white lintels, terminate at the nave floor and are covered in translucent glass. To increase the lighting level electric lights are added into the slots. The surface of the red bricks is scabbled to give a velvety texture to the arched walls. The semicircular end wall of the crypt, behind the altar, is faced by an arch of roughly hewn stones adding a further dimension to the moving and calm atmosphere of this unusual space. The staircase and adjacent corridors reveal additional typical Plečnik details such as freestanding stone balustrading infills, niches at the end of vistas, and grilles made of polished artificial stone cylinders. The main reason for building the crypt was the lack of side chapels in the main body of the church, and it fulfilled the requirement for intimate, secluded meditation and prayer.

49

50

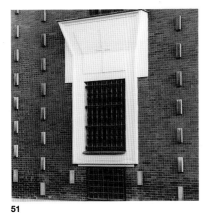

51

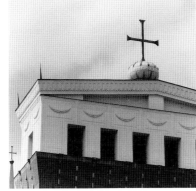

52

The inspiration for the shape of the crypt and its lighting slots possibly came from Plečnik's similar handling of the tunnel for the President's car at Prague Castle. Plečnik designed the tunnel just before he completed the final proposals for the church, and it leads from the third courtyard to the glazed circular lift up to the President's apartment.

A parish hall, however, planned as a separate building east of the main church and designed by Plečnik in the same architectural style as the nave, was never built due to a lack of funds.

Externally the church is enclosed up to the clerestory windows by attractive dark brown brickwork decorated at regular intervals with vertical rectangular pieces of grey granite. Before the brick coat reaches the top it cants outwards forming a kind of heavy collar or a massive cornice for the clerestory windows and roof to sit on. The heavy cornice is a typical element used by Cubist architects before the First World War and can be seen in Josef Chochol's and Antonín Belada's houses in Neklanova Street in Prague's Vyšehrad quarter. There the top cornices similarly crown the uppermost part of the buildings. Plečnik denied any such influences, although Czech architect Pavel Janák identified Plečnik's design for the reinforced concrete facade of the Stollwerk chocolate factory in Vienna from 1910 as an influential inspiration for the evolution of Czech Cubism in architecture.

Above the brick wall a totally different architecture of classical proportions and conception appears, faced, by contrast, in white render. Again the top cornice leans outwards repeating the notion from the detail below. This idea weighed the building down, but at the same time appeared to open up the wall enclosure of the house of God in a gesture of invitation to the heavens above. Now, however, the relief of the stuccowork is less pronounced than when originally executed, as the depth of modelling has been reduced over the years by renovation and paintwork.

The door portals also mimic the leaning of the cornice. In fact, Plečnik took this motif very effectively through all the major features and in this way successfully unified the composition. The architecture of the church exterior is a close reminder of Plečnik's earlier work, the Zacherl House, where the modern, clean conception of the plain granite-faced lower part of the building supports the more classical concept of the uppermost storey.

53

54

55

56

51, 52 The use of contrasting exterior materials emphasizes the main elements of the architecture of the church.
53 Josef Chochol's Cubist Hodek Apartment Building, Prague, 1913–14, with its massive cantilevered cornice.
54 Detail of a gable of another Cubist building by Chochol, 1912–13.
55, 56 Openings in the church's brick facade are framed in white render, clearly resembling Cubist architectural forms.

57

58

59

60

While Plečnik was designing the Vinohrady church he was also preoccupied with making proposals for costumes for the Catholic sports organization Orel. When returning to architecture Plečnik had in mind Gottfried Semper's views on textiles. Semper pointed out that the meaning of architecture was historically highlighted by the use of textiles. In his book, *Der Stil* (1860-63), he set out his theory on practical aesthetics, about colour in architecture and the important role of building cladding. Semper proposed that functional motifs could be transferred from one material to another and by doing so would assume symbolic significance.

It is not surprising, then, that the facing brick walls with the pieces of granite were likened by many observers to a regal ermine robe worn over a white garment, symbolized by the top storey. With this concept of the facade Plečnik meant to underline the importance of the Vinohrady church as a representative of the royal borough and its setting in a square named after a Czech King.[7] This treatment of the external walls was similar to methods used in Renaissance architecture and to Wagner's favourite detail of aluminium bolts fastening marble slabs to the facades of his buildings which were seen to have both a decorative and practical function.

The statues placed on the cantilevered stone pedestals above the entrance doors are later additions. Regretfully they sit awkwardly on the granite shelves and Plečnik would surely not have approved. The protracted delays in completing the fitting out of the building were due to the continued lack of money and changes to the political system of the country; thus the final touches were accomplished in the 1980s long after Plečnik's death in 1957 and without his guiding hand.

Realization of the church

In May 1928 all preliminary formalities were concluded, the ownership of the site confirmed and permission to build applied for. This was received at the beginning of October. On 28 October 1928, the tenth anniversary of the establishment of the Republic, the granite foundation stone inscribed MCMXXVIII 28.X. was consecrated.

However, neither the sale of Bepta's endowment had been completed nor the tender procedure finalized. Of the five builders who offered prices the Václav Nekvasil company from Prague-Karlín was the lowest at 2,448,289.28 Kč (£14,930 at contemporary rates) and, after offering to dispose of Karel Bepta's land parcels on behalf of the church, was chosen to proceed with the contract. All these activities delayed the start on site, and the first dig for the new foundations did not begin until 19 August 1929.

It was soon found that ground conditions were not favourable for the assumed foundation design; unwisely a soil survey had not been carried out before the contract had been let. A 1,600mm foundation raft was needed under the tower and deeper 600mm strip foundations had to carry the loadbearing walls, and a further 700,000 Kč was required. The Church Association had to find quickly the additional finances while work continued on site. The placing of concrete was completed by the beginning of 1930 by which time underground services could be laid, including drainage and electricity.

In August 1930, as the walls began to rise, Plečnik visited the site to discuss and oversee progress with his supervising architect, Otto Rothmayer. Further details were needed to complete the works and Plečnik obligingly supplied the necessary drawings free of charge. By October the nave roof structure was secured and in November the tower was under cover and the topping out ceremony could take place. By the end of 1930 the following quantities of materials had been used by the contractor: 6,200m³ of sand, 1,302,000 bricks, 8,250 tonnes of concrete, 85,000kg of steel reinforcement and 820m³ of timber.

1931 started with heavy frost and only interior work could be carried out such as electrical and plumbing installations. In March, the steel framework for the cross and orb was erected on top of the church tower, made by the Hatle firm of Prague to Plečnik's design. The orb, two and a half metres in diameter, was covered in copper sheeting and the cross, four and a half metres high, was also sheathed in copper. Gold-plated letters, IHS, and the date, MCMXXXI, were attached to the orb. With the idea of the orb Plečnik reinforced the royal image of the church.

61

The rendering of the upper part of the tower started in May and the timber ceiling of the nave was put in place together with other carpentry tasks. By summer the roof covering was completed and the clock received its glazed dials. An order for the main altar was placed with the firm Prastav, and was to be carved from Jarošovice marble.

In December 1931 President Masaryk visited the nearly completed church admiring the spatial nave and its timber ceiling. He was enthralled by the impression created by the crypt. Early the following year Masaryk wrote to Plečnik:

Dear Professor Plečnik,
I would like to tell you a few words about my visit to your Vinohrady church. The question and problems of the church have attracted me for some time: How should a church with its internal arrangement express the main idea of religion… I accept Christianity according to Jesus Christ's teachings and that is why I would picture the church as a space for the Sermon on the Mount: a spatial (non-Gothic) hall, with a slightly raised podium which would signify the mountain from which the priest would preach, in this way being seen and heard everywhere by everybody, and not standing on a column, near a wall… Your church is spacious, airy and I like that… I talk about the interior only. The exterior is a resolutely interesting experiment… You understand I do not want to exhaust the subject, there are many questions, mainly regarding the interior decorations, all about which we could talk…[8]

This was one of the more positive comments. As the church neared completion, several critiques appeared in a number of specialist periodicals and newspapers. Many were harsh and superficial claiming that the church was not artistic enough and rather plain. In opposition, important personalities, including the writer Karel Čapek, known worldwide for his plays *Rossum's Universal Robots* and *From the Life of the Insects*, supported Plečnik's work, seeing in it a significant contribution to Prague architecture. Furthermore, Dr Hrudka in the magazine *Stavitelské listy* (*Building News*), 1931, stated that:

Plečnik used only carefully processed Czech materials. Even a simple piece of matter is a gift of God, and similar abilities to engage in the process of work God endowed to man. To the service of God a man should give his best and Plečnik, without any reward, dedicated his efforts to the Vinohrady church for several years. This church is built on an artistic level especially for future generations, because the present one has not yet grown up to appreciate the form of this church. Even in the smallest details we feel the effort of a strong creative spirit…[9]

In February 1932 the main altar was delivered and installed including the marble lecterns on either side, which contained Plečnik's typical central column motif. Prastav was given the task of making the tabernacle, decorated with precious and semi-precious stones, and the sculpting of its guardian angels was carried out by Štěpán Zálesák. The dove symbol of the Holy Spirit on the tabernacle was created by Damian Pešan. Then, in April, the six church bells were brought to the site, ranging from the biggest at 3,620kg to the smallest weighing 40kg. After consecration the bells were placed in a single row at the top of the tower.

61 The main altar and tabernacle were designed by Plečnik and realized by Štěpán Zálesák and Damian Pešån in 1932.
62 Plečnik's marble lectern with the central column motif.
63 The side altars, designed by Otto Rothmayer, were made from Ostružín and Carrara marble.

62

63

64 A view of the altar from the side with Rothmayer's tall brass column lights, the tabernacle and gilded statues supported from the red brick wall.
65 The timber central entrance doors in the west wall.
66 The door's brass handle in the form of a cross.

64

65

66

Plečnik supplied further drawings for the altar light and the handles to the sacristy doors which were cast in brass by metalworker Karel Pešan. On 8 May 1932 the church, to great local celebrations and pageantry, was consecrated by Prague Archbishop Dr Kašpar. In memory of that day a marble plaque was inserted into the nave wall by the southwest entrance with the Latin inscription:

ECCLESIAM HANC IN HONOREM SS CORDIS JESU DIE VIII MAJI AD MCMXXXII CONSECRAVIT EXLMUS DNUS DR CAROLUS KASPAR ARCHIEPPUS PRAGEN.

However, the church interior decorations were still not completed and work continued. In spring 1934 the sculpture of the Sacred Heart, designed by Plečnik and carved by Pešan, was erected above the main altar.

Plečnik came to see the church for the last time in the autumn of 1934 and, from then on, Rothmayer took over responsibility for completion of the work, travelling to Ljubljana several times to see Plečnik and make sure that he agreed with his decisions. During one of Rothmayer's visits Plečnik offered a drawing of a circular timber chandelier, initially proposed for the Zacherl Chapel in Döbling, which was carved and then suspended above the main altar by Christmas 1935. By the following Christmas a new organ was made and installed by the Josef Mölzer company; and in 1938 stonemason Mrázek sculpted two fonts, to Plečnik's design, using dark Silesian marble.

Six statues depicting the Czech patron saints, by sculptor Damian Pešan, completed the main altar decorations where Plečnik originally envisaged only three statues. To the left of the Sacred Heart were arranged the statues of St Wenceslas, the Czech prince between 921-935, St Ludmila, his grandmother, and St Procopius. To the right were St Adalbert, the first Czech Bishop of Prague, St Agnes, the daughter of the Czech King Přemysl Otakar I, and St John Nepomuk.

67

68

The corner altars were supplied by Mrázek and made from Ostružín marble, and the six 3.5m high brass lights, designed by Rothmayer, were added to the main altar in October 1939. At the end of 1940 the corner altars received their statues of the Virgin Mary and St Joseph from sculptor A Berka.

Although the Second World War prevented contact with Plečnik, Rothmayer continued the works by proposing the two side altars which were made by Mrázek, again from Ostružín marble. However, the quarry could not cope with supplying for such large altar tables and Italian Carrara marble was used instead. Berka provided the statues of St Antony of Padua and St Theresa of Lisieux.

The Germans, who occupied Bohemia and Moravia from March 1939, confiscated all the church bells, except the smallest, melting them down for use in the war effort in March 1941. Tragically, the small community of dedicated church priests did not escape the German occupation with only this loss, for in June 1942 Father Zámečník was arrested by the Gestapo for allegedly not offering holy communion to a woman with a swastika badge on her coat. He was sent to Terezín and then to Dachau concentration camp where he died.

Soon after the end of the war, in 1948, the Communists took over the country and church activities were suppressed. The Church Association was therefore banned, and most of the priests were dismissed and had to find civilian employment. Nevertheless, the last statues, which were still missing, were slowly delivered to the church, and in 1950 a sculpture of the Good Shepherd, by Bedřich Stefan, was placed over the left entrance door. After a long wait the second statue of a Praying Woman was hoisted over the right-hand door in 1971. The statue of the Madonna and Child which was intended to go over the main door remained unfinished due to Stefan's early death; even so it was purchased in 1983 and set up above the central door. These delays perhaps explain the slightly unsatisfactory state of these artefacts in relation to the rest of the architecture.

One final problem had yet to be tackled. Due to the poor acoustic qualities of the main nave the priest could not be heard in many places; therefore, after a number of experiments with various devices, including the use of war-time equipment left behind during the occupation, the present solution of suspended globe-shaped speakers received approval from the congregation and priests. This equipment seemed to be the least obtrusive and in keeping with the design spirit of the holy building. In fact, Plečnik had envisaged this problem and originally planned to suspend a number of chandeliers from the steel roof trusses to break up the large space and improve the acoustics of the nave.

The Velvet Revolution of November 1989 brought renewed and unhindered religious activities and a few outstanding elements were resolved. Three new bells to complement the last remaining since the war are currently being ordered to be hung in the near future and a central-heating system has been installed. The new democratic society successfully established in the Czech Republic now enables free access to the building to all Catholics and those interested in the history of architecture and Plečnik's work.

67, 68 Either side of the main altar, two additional altars were positioned diagonally across the nave corners. The Virgin Mary stands in the southeast corner and St Joseph, on an identical Ostružín marble altar, is placed on the opposite side.
69 The gilded statue of St Agnes forms part of the main altar decoration.
70 The nave's dark, timber coffered ceiling complements the light terrazzo floor with its textile-inspired motifs.

69

70

71

71 The stone Lion Head
Fountain by Plečnik in the
President's apartment,
Prague Castle, 1922–27.
72 A granite bollard by
Plečnik at the entrance
to the Paradise Garden.
73 A large stone newel of the
Paradise Garden balustrade
confirming Plečnik's sensitivity in
handling materials and creating
unusual forms.

72

73

Plečnik's architecture

Many regard the Church of the Sacred
Heart as the culmination of Plečnik's work
since his subsequent, postwar projects and
realized buildings somehow lack the same
vitality, freshness and originality. This
church represents Plečnik's personality and
his ability to deal with material, colour, form
and massing in an individual way. He did
not consciously use or copy architectural
elements from the past, but rather adjusted,
remodelled and combined them to create
new features which could stand alone,
independently of the past. Plečnik did not
go back deliberately to history in order to
create something new for the present era;
for him the past *was* the present. Pavel
Janák, a great admirer of Plečnik and his
successor at Prague Castle, described
Plečnik as:

…the individual spirit of a man coming out
of himself and insisting on his own abilities.
He is not an artist living in the past, he is an
exception, and he is part of his era, because
his thinking lasts in his time with its strength
and content… Plečnik, although he uses
established stylistic forms, moves
unhindered, with freedom, and builds alone
the highest order, as secure as classicism
itself… In his art live columns, cornices, but
they are unlike anything from the past…
Plečnik's spirit and work move outside
the common direction, move somehow
independently, without the notion of time
and space…[10]

Otto Wagner required his students to
develop the practical as well as the artistic
aspects of architectural creativity: 'A thing
that is not practical cannot be beautiful' he
stressed.[11] In his book *Moderne Architektur*,
published in 1895, Wagner formulated the
idea that architects can find inspiration
from past tradition but must not copy from
it. The requirements of modern life will
inevitably remodel architecture since new
art cannot be purely the outcome of
'archaeological studies'.[12] The architect's
work has to be based on what was living
and immediate and has to assess the
requirements of modern man. 'Architecture
has an immense power to affect people,
literally compelling them to look at it, and
for that reason it may be said to be the most
powerful of all arts.'[13]

These impulses formed Plečnik's
creativity during his studies, and with
his projects Plečnik endorsed Wagner's
dictum which emphasized that all elements
must have functional requirements and
these must be fulfilled completely. In
addition, however, Plečnik endowed his
buildings with a deep spiritual sense.

Apart from Wagner's teachings, the
writings of the German architect Gottfried
Semper (1803–79) greatly influenced
Plečnik's thinking and work, and his
revolutionary theories are clearly reflected
in Plečnik's buildings. Semper identified
three attributes to the idea of the formal
beauty of art and architecture: symmetry,
proportion and direction, with one of these
always more dominant than the other two.
Moreover Semper defined a fourth
attribute, the most important one
supporting the other three: that of
the quality of content or purpose.

74

Semper's philosophy elevated the concept of idea above all other architectural considerations including material: 'The material, though essential, is in no way the first and most important coefficient to affect the configuration of architectural forms. Material must conform to the idea; the idea must not evolve out of the material…'[14] This attitude stressed the importance of the intellectual content of architectural creativity which Plečnik wholeheartedly adopted, and in analysing Plečnik's buildings we can find, though sometimes deep under the surface, the attributes espoused by Semper.

The content or purpose unifies the elements to form the main point of the work, creating the expression and character of the building. Semper's other notion, that the whole configuration should be arranged in such a way that the relationship to the surrounding environment is expressed as clearly as possible to radiate an impression of rest, permanence and perfection, gave Plečnik further guidance. Furthermore, Plečnik confirmed his respect for Semper in the design of the Lion Head Fountain at the President's apartment at Prague Castle. Below the animal's head (the twin-tail lion being the heraldic animal on the Bohemian crest) is engraved plainly in large letters the word SEMPER, here endowed with a double meaning, first as 'always' in Latin, and secondly as Plečnik's own subtle tribute to Semper.

Plečnik believed that true art and architecture could only be attained through hard work and total dedication. He founded his work on a strict moral basis and religious spiritual force and all major decisions had to fulfil that given framework, which would perhaps explain Plečnik's attitude towards non-secular projects and his refusal to accept payment for that work. His motivation was to create a better world by achieving harmony between spiritual and materialistic environments.

Plečnik's efforts at Prague Castle consisted of small, precise architectural and symbolic elements – a granite container, a monolith, a fountain, a staircase and copper canopy, a pyramid – most of these arranged and connected in a horizontal direction and radiating enormous strength and power which is easier to understand once Semper's influence is appreciated. The underlying force of Plečnik's creativity is clearly recognizable against the background of the historic Castle buildings and landscape. Such power is inevitably diluted in a large complex building like the Vinohrady church, which is perceived with difficulty in one simple glance or view, and has to be appreciated with care, time and attention to capture all the subtleties Plečnik tried to put before us.

74 A massive container by Plečnik carved from one piece of Mrákotín granite and supported on two small granite blocks, Paradise Garden, 1920–27.
75 A stone amphora displayed elegantly in a wall niche, another typical Plečnik motif in the Paradise Garden.
76 An attractive wall fountain at the foot of the steps in the Paradise Garden by Plečnik.

75

76

77

78

79

According to Wagner a building
is not a natural phenomenon but a
system contrived by human creativity.
Even a calm view of a building is always
charged with tension and movement.
When a person walks towards, through
or around a building he performs a highly
complex mental act, in which he creates,
at every stage along his way, a new image
of the building, which then serves him as
a system of reference for his movements.[15]

The Church of the Sacred Heart is a
perfect architectural symbol expressing all
the inner feelings and abilities of Plečnik.
Sitting faultlessly in the square, the church's
form combines with the local urban
structure and traditions, and yet it is so
unusual and different from other
architectural work in the city and elsewhere.
It was typical of Plečnik to create an
individual and singular building every time;
he never repeated his architectural designs
but varied the outcome with the skill of an
accomplished and unique artist.

Protagonists of post-modernism regard
Plečnik as their mentor and predecessor;
however, Plečnik never spoke the same
language. The recent architectural trend
dwelling superficially in the past, without
deep spiritual content, cannot compare
its attitudes and existence to Plečnik's
meticulously determined work. In post-
modernism the past forms, elements and
symbols are placed together and arranged
in architectural compositions
with exuberant attitude and without any
sign of philosophical or moral criteria.
The architecture of this trend can be seen
as reflecting the prime intent of its creators
to elevate the importance of their
personality above the unpretentious art
of building design.

Plečnik's approach, by contrast, was
wholly encompassing and carefully planned
to the last detail, and his attitude was based
on intellectual, religious and personal
involvement in order that his architecture
contained meaningful and truly believed
ideas and concepts. Plečnik was convinced
of his purpose to achieve the utmost which
could be attained in the art of architecture
and shared this skill with others by
displaying his work to the widest audience.
Otakar Novotný defined Plečnik's legacy in
1958, a year after his death, by assessing
correctly its value for future generations:
'We are able to taste Plečnik's work as if it
were consecrated with the highest attribute
of which architecture is capable, but it is not
work which it will be possible to follow.'[16]

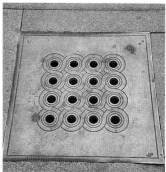

80

The exterior of the church trans-
forms with the time of day, light
falling on its facade creating a
moving and magical impression.
The building's appearance is
constantly changing as materials
and finishes alter in colour and
texture.

The west facade is dominated
by three entrances, dramatically
framed by rendered portals
resembling the backs of
priests' robes; proof of
Semper's influence in his
textile references to architectural
design and Plečnik's readiness
to try these ideas.

Materials, surface textures and colours contribute significantly in defining the architectural elements of the exterior composition. The window surrounds repeat the shape of the canted cornice holding this family of forms together.

Above The succession of cornices to the nave and tower show almost identical treatment and design.
Right The clock and bell tower stands high above the surrounding urban landscape clearly locating the church within Prague's panorama.
Overleaf The massive tower is lightened by the insertion of large circular openings housing the transparent clock faces. Inside, a daring Modernist access walkway to the clock and the bells spans the glazed dials, minimizing its impact.

Left Slender pyramids either side of the main tower contribute to the dynamic quality of the composition. They replaced the four originally designed brick columns which would have appeared slightly alien to the rest of the architecture.

Above and right The sharp edges of forms are reinforced by copper spikes, crosses and a royal orb at the top of the clock and bell tower.

Overleaf The wide nave is simple and subdued, generating a Mediterranean atmosphere and character.

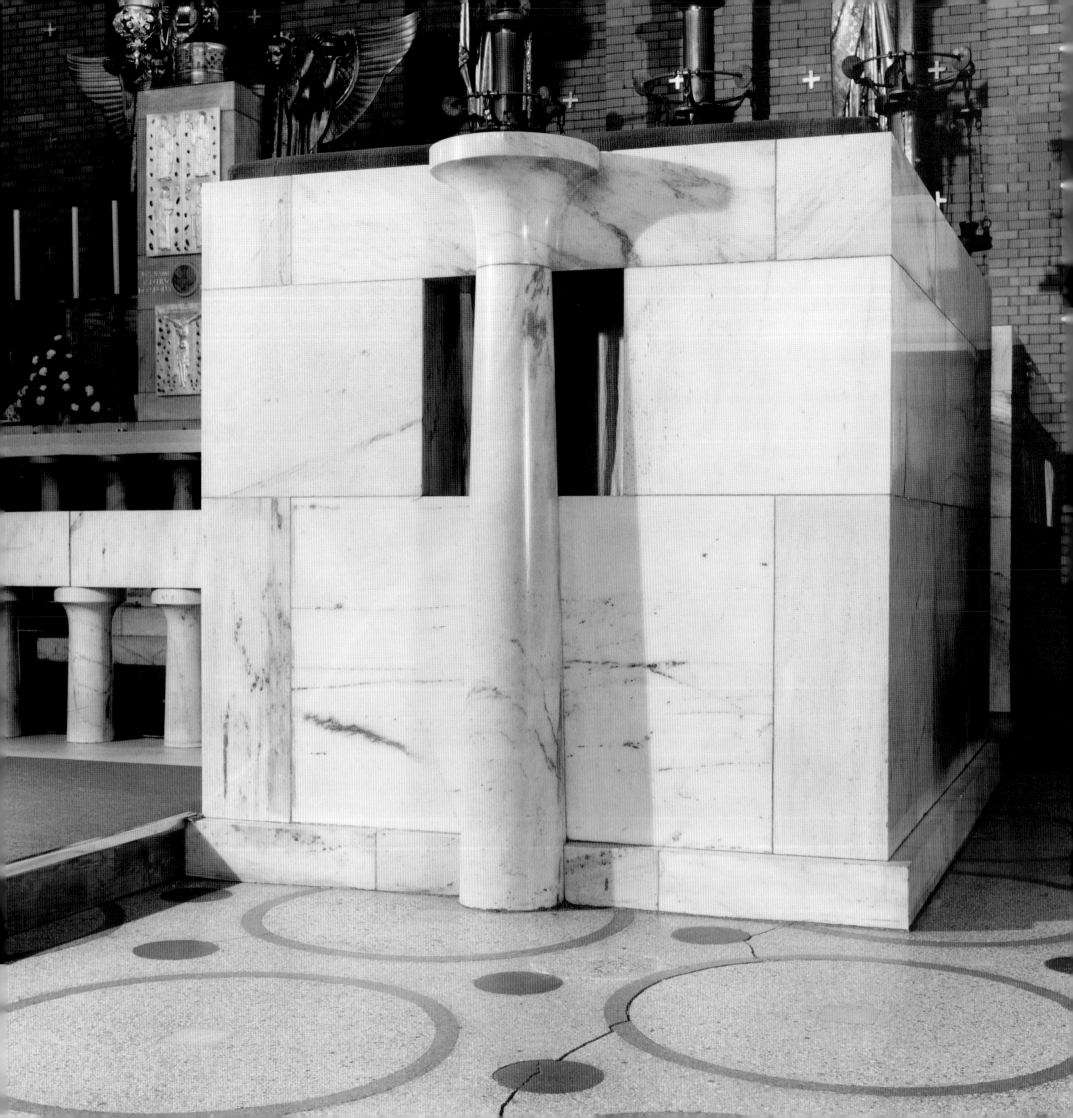

Left The Ostružín marble
lecterns display Plečnik's
signature of a centrally placed
column.

Above and right The light
marble altar and tabernacle
contrasts with the dark brickwork, while surrounding gilded
statues provide an appropriate
and dignified air to the nave.

Left, above and right The unusual corner altars and side altars, designed by Rothmayer, carry the theme of the central support. The clerestory stained glass windows with Christian symbols colour the light reaching the nave interior.
Far right The corner altar of the Virgin Mary.

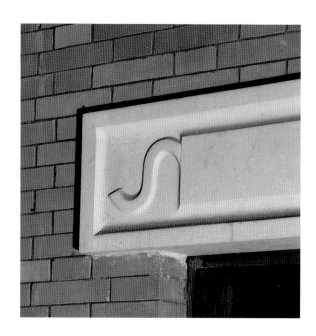

All the major door openings are bridged by stone lintels which have decorative carvings.

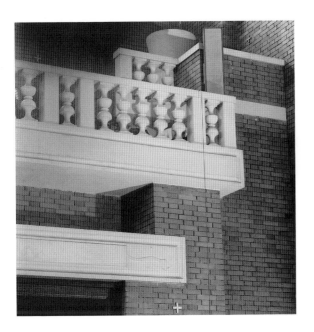

The Modernist access walkway
to the clerestory windows
contrasts with the classical
balustrade of the organ gallery
on the west wall (above).

Left The crypt is a well defined
space that makes an immediate
and emotional impact.
Above Axes are concluded by
niches and corridor steps fan out
elegantly into wider spaces
announcing their presence and
guiding the visitor.

Location plan

1 Church of the Sacred Heart

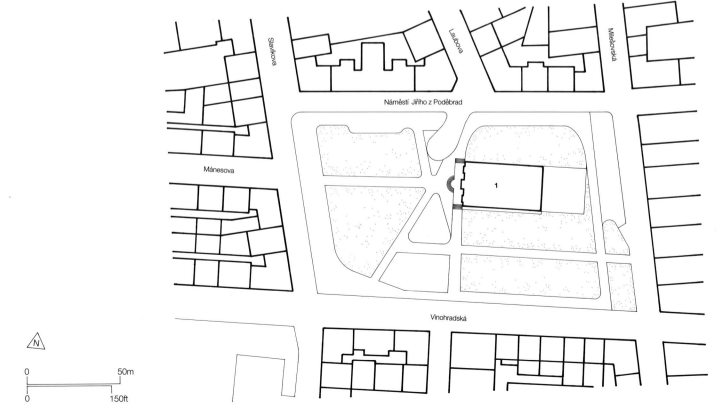

Slavíkova

Laubova

Milešovská

Námĕstí Jiřího z Poděbrad

Mánesova

1

Vinohradská

N

0 — 50m

0 — 150ft

Floor plans

1 crypt
2 cellar
3 store
4 entrance terrace
5 narthex
6 nave
7 altar
8 crossing beneath clock tower
9 baptism hall
10 sacristy
11 east entrance

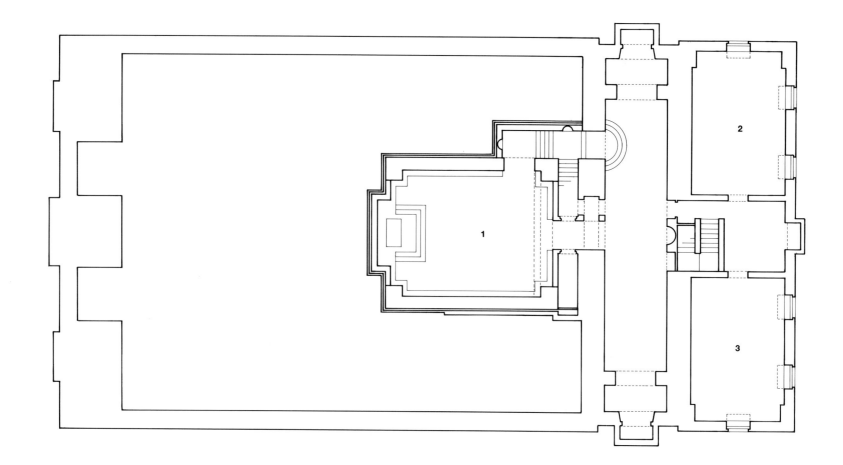

Basement plan

0   5m

0   15ft

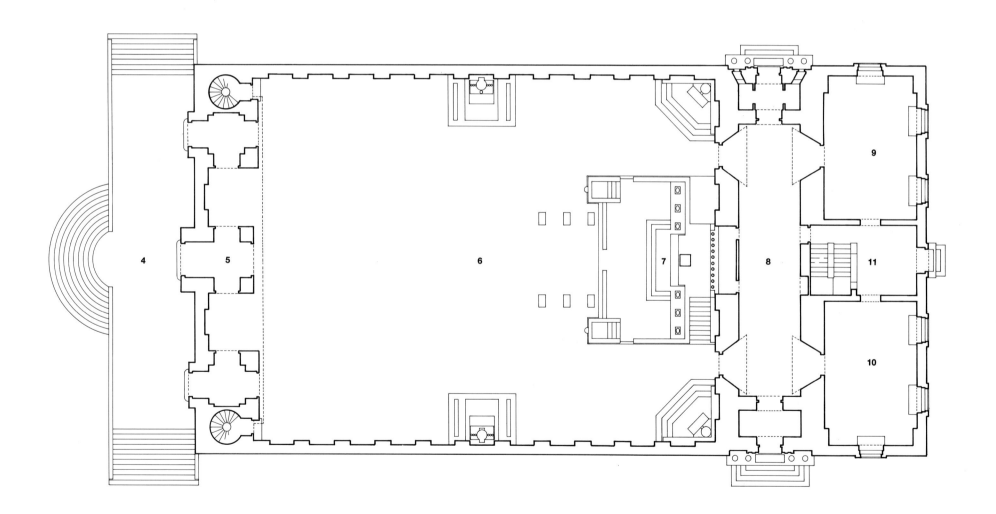

Ground-floor plan

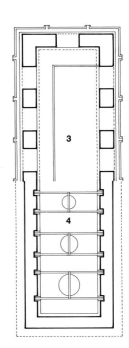

Plan of tower

Floor plans

1 organ and choir gallery
2 store
3 clock tower
4 bells

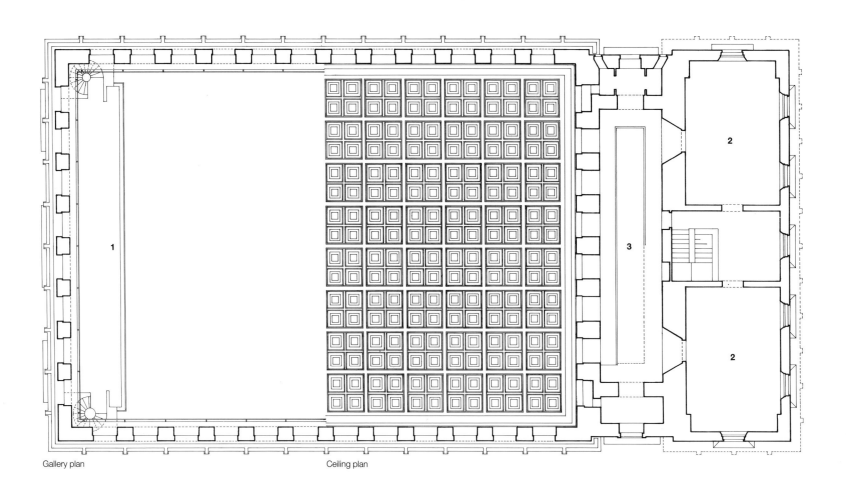

Gallery plan

Ceiling plan

0   5m

0   15ft

West elevation

0   5m

0   15ft

East elevation

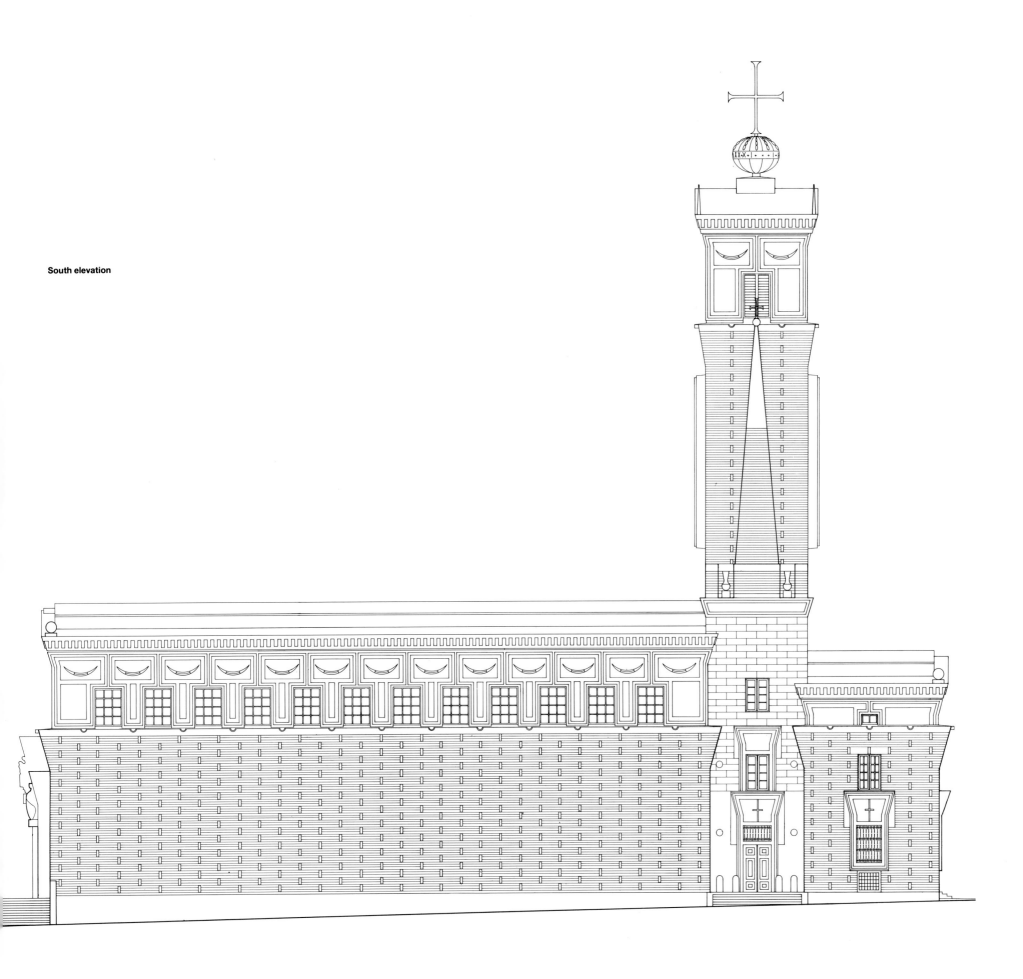

South elevation

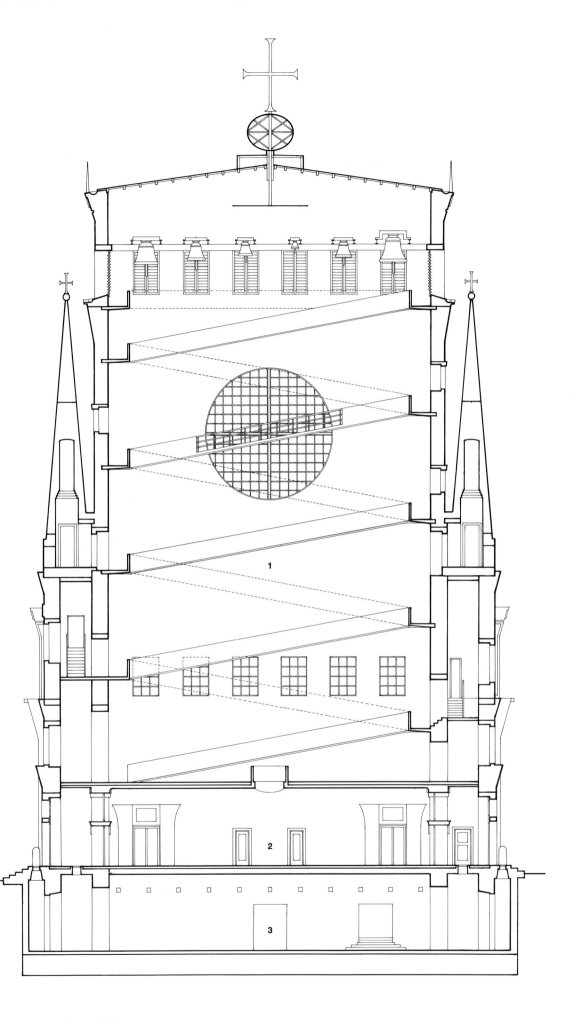

Sections

1 clock tower
2 crossing beneath clock tower
3 crypt
4 cellar
5 store
6 baptism hall
7 sacristy
8 nave
9 organ and choir gallery
10 crypt

0   5m

0   15ft

Cross section through tower looking west

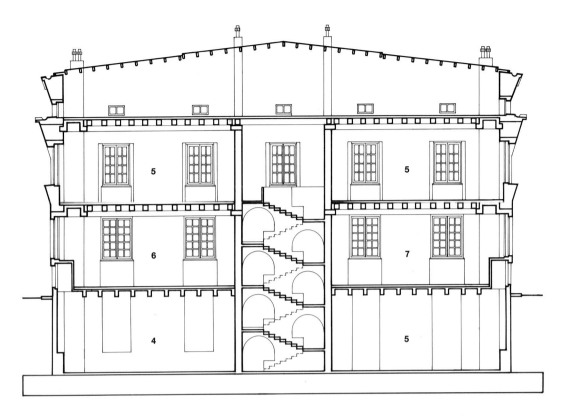

Cross section through sacristy looking east

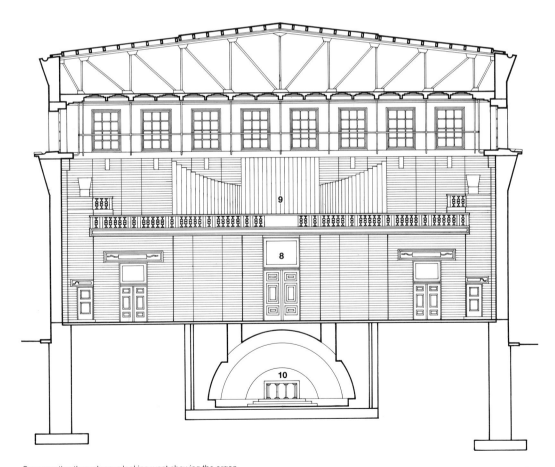

Cross section through nave looking west showing the organ
as originally proposed by Plečnik

Sections

1 altar
2 crypt
3 nave
4 entrance terrace
5 narthex
6 crossing beneath clock tower
7 clock tower
8 mezzanine
9 stair

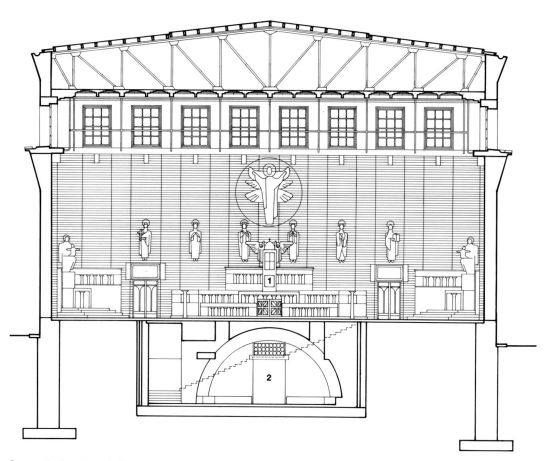

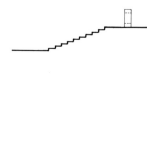

Cross section through nave looking east showing two windows
above the main altar that were excluded in the final construction

Longitudinal section

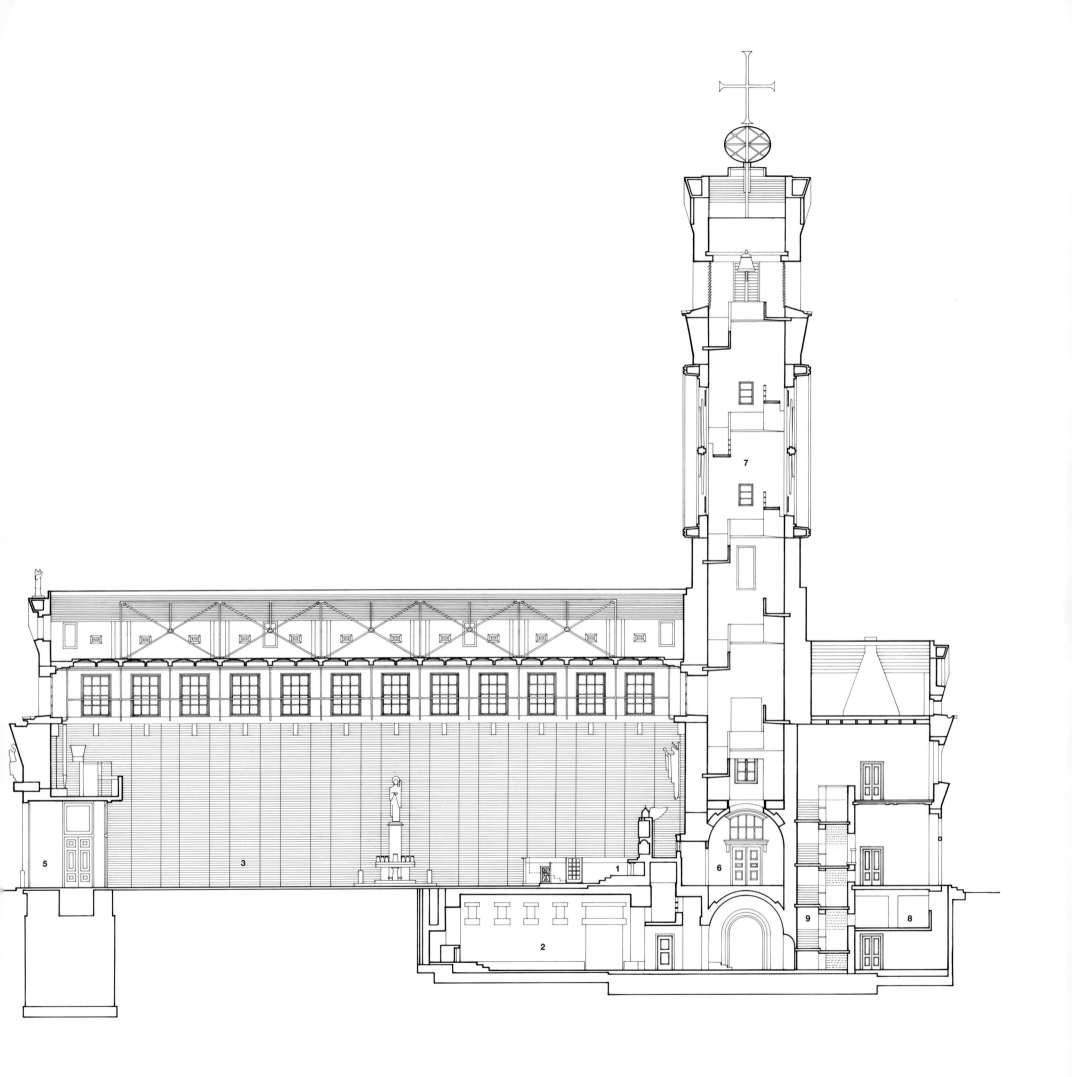

Author's acknowledgements

I would like to thank Dr Peter Krečič from the Arhitekturni Muzej, Ljubljana and Dr Damjan Prelovšek for supplying materials from their archives; MUDr Jiří Slabý for revealing all the available information about the church and Plečnik in Prague; Ing arch Zdeněk Lukeš for showing Plečnik's work at Prague Castle; Ing arch Petr Krajči from the National Technical Museum, Prague for copies of contemporary articles; Amanda Bates for help and support; Heda Margolius Kovály for translations and advice; and Roy White for comments and suggestions.

Illustration acknowledgements

Black and white referential illustrations have been provided courtesy of the following: Arhitekturni Musej, Ljubljana: figs 1, 3, 70; Edvard Primožič: figs 4, 26. All other photographs courtesy of Mark Fiennes or the author.

Notes

1
Kotěra, J, *Volné směry*, Vol 6, 1902, p 91.

2
Plečnik's letter to Kotěra dated 3 September 1910 in the archive of the National Technical Museum, Prague.

3
Novotný, O, *Jan Kotěra a jeho doba* (Praha: SNKLHU, 1958), p 43.

4
Plečnik's letter to Father Škarda, dated 25 October 1918, quoted in Prelovšek, D, *Josef Plečnik 1857–1957: Architectura perennis* (Salzburg: Residenz Verlag, 1992), p 229.

5
Quoted in Burkhardt, F, C Eveno, and B Podrecca, *Jože Plečnik, Architect: 1872–1957* (Cambridge, Mass: MIT Press, 1989), pp 92, 94. The letter is kept at the Plečnik Museum, Ljubljana.

6
Prelovšek, D, *op cit*, p 233.

7
See for example, Hrudka, Dr V, 'Plečnikův Chrám na Král. Vinohradech', *Stavitelské listy*, Vol 27, 1931, p 362.

8
T G Masaryk's letter to Plečnik is dated 23 January 1932, quoted in Ondráš, Dr F and R Pavlíčková, *Chrám Nejsvětějšího Srdce Páně 1932–1992*, Praha, 1992, pp 19–20.

9
Hrudka, Dr V, *op cit*, p 365.

10
Janák, P, Josef Plečnik v Praze, *Volné směry*, Vol 26, 1927, pp 97–108.

11
Wagner, O, *Die Baukunst unserer Zeit*, 4th edition of *Moderne Architektur* (Vienna: Anton Schroll, 1914), p 44.

12
Wagner, O, *Moderne Architektur*, 2nd edition, (Vienna: Anton Schroll, 1899), p 36.

13
Wagner, O, *op cit*, p 16.

14
Semper, G, Preface to *Vergleichende Baulehre*, 1849–50.

15
Wagner, O, *Die Baukunst unserer Zeit*, p 43.

16
Novotný, O, *op cit*, p 43.

Chronology

1908
The decision is made to build a second Catholic church in the Královské Vinohrady borough and a site is given to the church administration.

1911
Plečnik comes to Prague to teach at the Institute of Decorative Arts.

1914
Foundation of an Association for the Construction of the Second Catholic Church at Královské Vinohrady.

1919
Anonymous architectural competition for the second Catholic church is held by the Association. Association of Czech Architects offers the church project to Plečnik.

1921
Plečnik leaves Prague to teach at University of Ljubljana. Plečnik proposes conversion of St Alois' chapel.

1922
Plečnik produces the first design for the church and an option with an alternative facade treatment.

1925
Plečnik submits his second scheme.

1927
The third and final scheme is sent by Plečnik to the Association.

1928
Foundation stone is consecrated on 28 October.

1929
Work on site starts in August under the supervision of Otto Rothmayer.

1930
Topping out ceremony is held in November.

1931
Fitting out of the church interior continues.

1932
In May the church is consecrated by Prague Archbishop Dr Kašpar.

1933
The crypt is completed.

1934
Plečnik visits the church for the last time. Work continues under supervision of Otto Rothmayer.

1938
All main altar statues are completed.

1940
The corner altars are in place with their statues.

1941
The church bells are confiscated by the Germans.

1950
The sculpture of the Good Shepherd is erected over the left entrance.

1971
The Praying Woman is placed over the right entrance.

1983
Finally the Madonna and Child is set above the central door.

Bibliography

Andrews, R M, I Bentley, D Grzan-Butina, *Jože Plečnik 1872–1957: Architecture and the City*, Oxford Polytechnic, 1983

Burkhardt, F, C Eveno and B Podrecca, *Jože Plečnik, Architect: 1872–1957* (Cambridge, Mass: MIT Press, 1989)

Geretsegger, H and M Peintner, *Otto Wagner 1841-1918* (London: Pall Mall Press, 1970)

Herrmann, W, *Gottfried Semper – In Search of Architecture* (Cambridge, Mass, and London: MIT Press, 1984)

Iz ljubljanske šole za architekturo, Ljubljana, 1925

Janák, P, *Vybrané stati autorovy* (Praha: UPM, 1985)

Krečič, P, *Plečnik – The Complete Works* (New York: Whitney, 1993)

Lučine. Iz ljubljanske šole za architekturo, Ljubljana, 1928

Lukeš, Z, 'Josip Plečnik a Pražský hrad', *Technický magazín*, Praha, 1991

Novotný, O, *Jan Kotěra a jeho doba*, (Praha: SNKLHU, 1958)

Ondráš, Dr F and R Pavlíčková, *Chrám Nejsvětějšího Srdce Páně 1932–1992*, Praha, 1992

Plečnik, J, *Výběr prací školy pro dekorativní architekturu v Praze z roku 1911–1921*, Praha, 1927

Prelovšek, D, *Josef Plečnik 1857–1957: Architectura perennis* (Salzburg: Residenz Verlag, 1992)

Prelovšek, D, Jože Plečnik, 'Gli interni del castello di Praga (1921–28)', *Domus*, April 1993

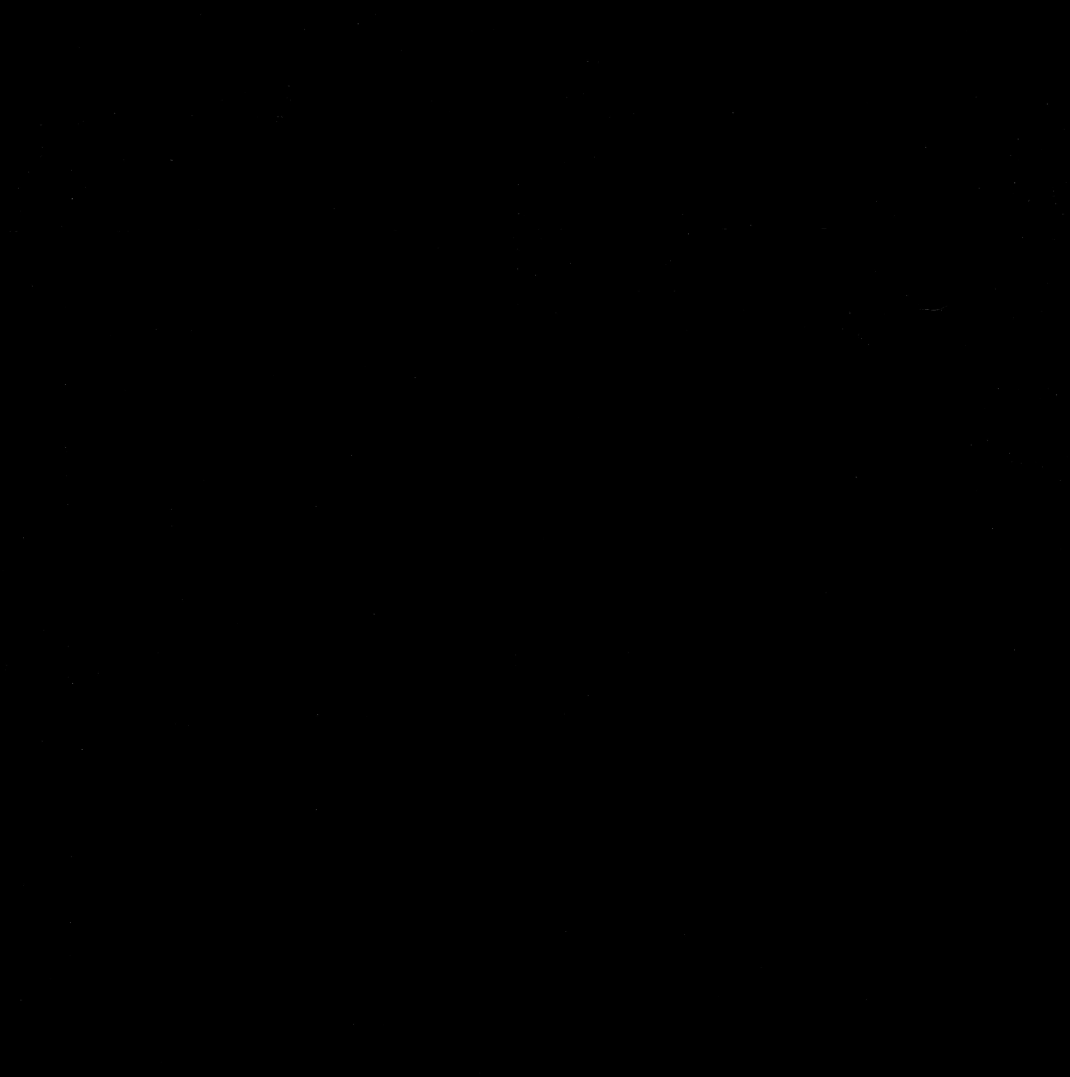

Tadao Ando
Church on the Water
Hokkaido, Japan 1988
Church of the Light
Osaka, Japan 1989

Philip Drew

Photography
Tadao Ando; Shinkenchiku-sha;
cover detail also by Shinkenchiku-sha
Drawings
Tadao Ando Architects and Associates

From the heartland of Japan

Tadao Ando is very physical person. He is continually animated. When talking to you his hands move constantly; suddenly he will pick up a coloured pencil and start to sketch. He is restless and compact – like a boxer in the ring he keeps moving. Ando's eyes smile back at you; they dance around you as though sparring and then reach out and clasp you momentarily as if to weigh you up, taking you in a grip that feels almost physical it is so intensely focused. Tadao Ando has a certain closeness, he experiences things and people in a tactile way.

Some people keep their distance when they meet new people. Not so Ando – he advances toward you. He is both centred and lively and his architecture can be thought of in the same way: his buildings instantly engage you, there is no way to avoid a response, they are so strongly formed, such insistent tectonic constructions. The walls, floors and ceilings, with their carefully placed openings and slots, are simultaneously metaphysical as well as physical instruments of his architecture.

It comes as no surprise to learn that Tadao Ando began his adult life as a boxer.

He is still boxing, only now he throws up walls the way some fighters throw punches. His walls hit you with the force and precision of a well-placed blow, and draw a clear boundary around his buildings. They are more than a barrier between inside and outside, for this isolation of the interior from the exterior marks a beginning not an ending. Ando's bounded domain is a very human space which assists people to develop and to be themselves.

From boxing, Ando learned that surprise gives a fighter an important advantage. This is something he shares with Alvar Aalto, who, when young, learned from a street-fighter friend the value of catching an opponent off guard. Indeed, one of Aalto's mottoes was, 'take them by surprise' – that is, always do the unexpected. Aalto turned the element of surprise into a lifelong architectural strategy. For Ando, the boxer turned architect, surprise is more than just a habit, it is a plan for dealing with design problems.

Osaka, Ando's home, is Japan's second largest city after Tokyo, and much older. Osaka borders the Inland Sea in the Setouchi-Kinki or Kinki region. This was the first area to be developed and is the heart-

1

1 The calm of Tadao Ando's architecture is belied by his physical presence – he is an intensely energetic and mentally focused individual and this shows immediately.
2 Osaka, Japan's second largest, is a sprawling giant without an obvious centre.
3 Tokyo, by comparison, is chaos with a still centre as its focus.

2

3

4

5

4 Tokyo never stops: at night, a blaze of neon signs, traffic, create a bizarre world of bars, clubs and restaurants, as work gives way to pleasure.
5 The Osaka skyline is generally flatter than in Tokyo, its tight grid of streets produces a dense horizontal matrix of buildings, a uniform chaos interrupted by expressways.
6 The seventeenth-century Yoshimura House: its elegant arrangement of white rectangular panels within dark timber frames, integrity of material, and subtle adjustment of daylight is close to Ando's architecture.
7 Light filtering through the high window of the nineteenth-century Habakino House makes us aware of the emptiness within.

land of Japan. Kyoto and Nara are close by: Kyoto is 45km to the north–northeast with Nara just 30km to the east. Whereas Tokyo was the city of the warrior and the Shogun, the Meiji and Emperor, and is now the centre of government, Osaka continues to be a city of merchants. It began as a fortified city and developed, mainly because of its central position with regard to sea traffic, into the commercial and industrial hub of Japan. Whereas Tokyo assumed a circular shape around Nihonbashi and the castle with the streets extending radially from the centre, Osaka, by contrast, followed the ancient Chinese system of rectangular blocks. The merchants' houses were concentrated near the harbour indicating the importance of sea trade. It is now a city of endless rows of factories and frenetic activity. The 1989 film *Black Rain* showed it at its raw and ugly worst.

Working in Osaka, Ando enjoys greater freedom than he might in Tokyo. Architecture in Tokyo is often arbitrary and just a little crazy. It frequently seems outrageous, being calculated to attract the eye in a city where buildings compete for attention and where anything odd or bizarre has a distinct

advantage. This jumping to extremes is all to do with the competition to be first, with everyone racing to catch the next wave; yet it is a race in which no one is quite sure what that next wave is likely to be about – and like so much else in Japanese life the winning post is continually shifting. Architects read constantly and watch one another. None of the architects knows for certain the general direction in which they should be travelling, so they run around in circles looking for it. Tadao Ando in Osaka is removed from this competition, and this freedom is precisely what makes him special. Moreover, Ando is a very self-reliant person.

Even as a child, Ando came into contact with the great classics of minka and traditional Japanese architecture. The magnificent seventeenth-century Yoshimura House at Habakino in Osaka Prefecture is not far away from the architect's practice. Without even being aware of it, Ando was exposed to this older tradition. This is apparent in his symbolic reliance on the wall and his preference for architectural compositions based on simple arrangements of squares.

6

7

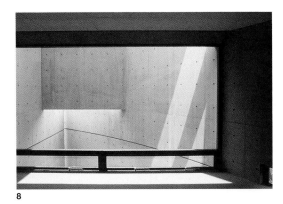

8

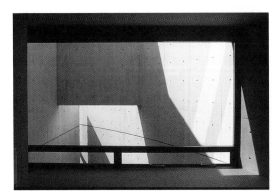

9

8, 9 Ando's Oyodo atelier: the
interiors of Ando's buildings are
continually changing, depending
on the day, the season, with the
shifting play of light patterns.
10 This futuristic twin tower by
architect Hiroshi Hara, in a style
recalling Sant' Elia, was intended
to give Osaka an appropriately
dynamic symbolic focus.
11 Ito House, Tokyo, 1990.
The protecting wall penetrates
the main volume of the building
in the form of a half-circle arc,
defining the entry space of
the house.

As an architect, Ando is self-taught; he never studied at a university school of architecture. For a short time he was apprenticed to a carpenter, but in 1962, he set out on travels that took him to the USA, Europe and Africa, which lasted until 1969. It was during these formative years of travel that he took to looking for the same qualities in the architecture of the West he had earlier encountered in Japanese farmhouses and townhouses. What had impressed him most was the effect of light filtering through the high windows into farmhouses in the snowy north of Japan. The sharp contrast of light and shade in the streets of medieval Italian cities reignited this memory. It revealed to Ando a richly realized world of unadorned forms and architectural spaces in which there was a real intimacy with the lives of ordinary people.

Ando's rise to prominence has been rapid. Many factors have been at work but one in particular helped considerably. Kenneth Frampton, a comparatively new Professor at Columbia University and the architectural adviser for the publisher Rizzoli in New York, became aware of Ando's architecture in the early 1980s, at about the same time that he was advancing his arguments on 'critical regionalism'. From this point of view, few other architects were better placed to illustrate his thesis, and Ando's architecture thus provided an exemplary demonstration of Frampton's ideas.

What most concerned Frampton was the worldwide spread of a mediocre homogeneous architecture by means of a phenomenon of universalization that signified not only a subtle destruction of traditional culture, but also represented an attack on the creative nucleus of the great cultures that form the basis of our interpretation of life itself.[1] Frampton was searching for something that would mediate the impact of a universal civilization with elements indirectly derived from the peculiarities of each region. He thought this would be made possible by, '… such things as the range and quality of the local light, or in a tectonic derived from a peculiar structural mode, or in the topography of a given site.'[2] Frampton stressed the importance of establishing a clearly bounded domain. He considered he might best resist the

10

11

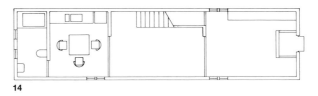
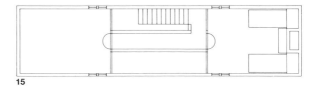

12 Matsutani House, Kyoto, 1978. This house by Ando was an attempt to create pure architectural space; compositionally, it consists simply of two blocks separated by a courtyard.
13 Azuma House, Sumiyoshi, Osaka, 1975–6. On the outside, Ando has repeated the facade unit of the existing row houses, while inside, the space is divided into two cubic blocks with a courtyard in between, connected by a bridge.
14–17 Azuma House plans, section and axonometric.

12

13

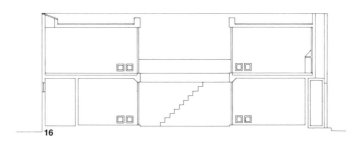

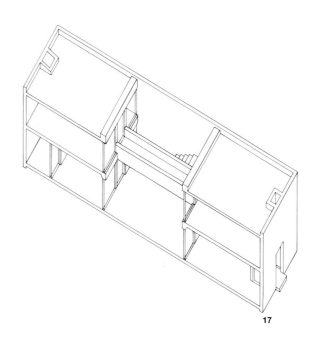

17

universalizing effects of technology by emphasizing the particular qualities of place-form and by invoking the capacity of the human body to read the environment in ways other than the visual.

In his book *Modern Architecture: A Critical History*,[3] Frampton lamented the fact that modern architecture suffered from a 'distancing' from its environment: 'This self-imposed limitation relates to that which Heidegger has called a "loss of nearness".'

Frampton's arguments almost perfectly meshed with what Ando was then doing. Ando's early work, after he opened his office in 1969, consisted principally of small houses built in the Kansai District and quickly came to reflect the regional vernacular of the area. This regional strain in the work was quite unconscious but nonetheless apparent, and nowhere was this more so than in his 1975–6 Row, or Azuma, House at Sumiyoshi, which was subsequently awarded the 1979 annual prize of the Architectural Institute of Japan.

Through his prolific writings, Frampton gained wide international recognition for Ando's achievements; and although It would be unfair to Ando to infer this was the

sole factor at work, it undoubtedly helped. In 1985 Ando received the Alvar Aalto Medal; then, in 1989, the French Academy of Architects honoured him with its Gold Medal; and this was followed in 1992 by the Carlsberg Architectural Prize from Denmark.

The secular and the sacred

The Church on the Water and Church of the Light were designed in the years between 1985 and 1988. Building work did not start until mid-1988: the Church on the Water was completed very quickly in five months; the construction of Church of the Light taking eleven months. The Chapel on Mount Rokko, near Kobe, Hyogo, in 1985–6, preceded them. These are mature works, coming after the international recognition signalled by the Alvar Aalto Medal. The two churches explore the dimension of sacred space, and appear different, yet their differences are more apparent than real. Before 1980, the majority of Tadao Ando's work had consisted of small houses. These were mainly of a closed spatial type, although there were some that were open, and a few that mixed the two spatial orientations. The houses of the late 1970s gradually acquired – almost reluctantly it might be suggested – an outward orientation that left open the possibility of eventually establishing a connection with the surrounding urban environment, without in the least bit compromising their essential centripetal character.[4] Indeed, Ando invested the secular private domain with aspects of the sacred.

Ando's work springs from the subconscious and finds an affinity with Zen philosophies while it is also connected with a deeper current in Japanese tradition. Through his work, Tadao Ando expresses the dual nature of existence. At the intersection of light and silence we become aware of 'nothingness', a void at the heart of things. Ando's houses, including his secular works, have this sacred quality which is more pronounced still in his church buildings.

One of the leading features of Ando's interiors is their profound emptiness. This can be disturbing at first, challenging as well as puzzling. The spaces have an unmistakable quality of poverty and stillness which is another way of describing tranquility. It is tempting to think of this as inspired by Ando's interest in modern architecture since a kind of spatial emptiness also arises in the two dimensional abstract pictorial spaces of Elementarism. In Tadao Ando's architecture 'emptiness' means something different, however – it introduces us to the spiritual dimension, to the 'Godhead'.

In Zen, and Zen art, 'being' is considered to be the self-unfolding of the unformed 'Nothing' or 'God'. In particular, the function of the beautiful is to spark an epiphany of the absolute and formless void which is God. True emptiness is the state of zero. This is expressed by the equation zero equals infinity, and vice-versa. Accordingly, emptiness is not literally a lack of content or passivity. It is 'being', and it is 'becoming'. It is knowledge and innocence. In architecture this means that perfect poverty is attained when perfect emptiness attains perfect fullness. Or, to put it another way: when 'nothing' becomes 'everything'.

As a piece of logic this is contradictory. It is only when we ourselves experience the richness of emptiness directly in spaces such as the Church on the Water and the Church of the Light that the psychological reality implicit in the assertion is fully registered.

18

18 Ando's Rokko Housing, 1981, is built against a steep hillside to the north of and overlooking Kobe.
19 Each apartment looks out across a south-facing terrace towards Kobe and the Inland Sea.
20 The housing is embedded in the mountainside with a street running up the centre from the bottom to the top.
21 Walkways at each level link the apartments to the central street.

20

21

19

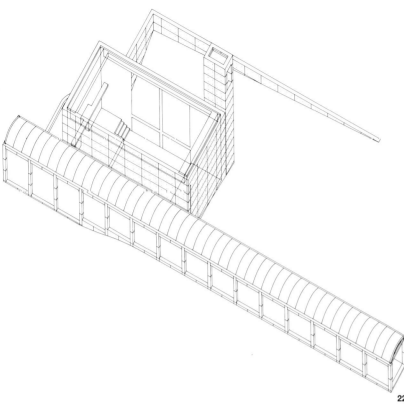

22

23

Because the Godhead is defined in Zen as a flowing together of all things in the 'nothing', in this equation, 'suchness' coincides with 'emptiness'. However, 'nothing' in this context is the precise opposite of the nihilism with which it is often confused in the West. On the contrary, Ando treats emptiness as a kind of divine fullness which is absolutely life-affirming. He is concerned with an inwardly echoing aesthetic poverty, a quality of simplicity which is encapsulated in the Japanese term *wabi*.

Ando's architecture reveals that the kind of emptiness he creates is intended to focus our vision by the elimination of anything extraneous which might divert our attention from what he sees as most real – that is, the essential quality of the space. Paring away his architecture in this way, reducing it to the simplest of terms, using a simple geometry of cubes and cylinders, bare concrete walls, solids and voids, light and darkness, Ando hopes to confront us with emptiness, with the Godhead. This is as true of his secular buildings as it is of the two churches. Light is the special medium which he uses to clarify the emptiness in his architecture.

The cosmic cube
The two churches represent a climax in which certain themes, present to some degree in most of Ando's work, are highlighted; in his terms, dwelling is not something separate but is inextricably linked to the sacred. Both church and house require the creation of a fixed point – a centre from which we orientate ourselves in the world, from which we go forth, and to which we return. Setting aside space, wresting the sacred from the mundane, requires that certain conditions are fulfilled. This notion finds a parallel in the opposition between inhabited territory and the unknown and indeterminate realm around it. The house resembles our own world, a cosmos, outside of which is chaos. This notion is fundamental to Ando's architecture. The Japanese city is a disorderly territory; it represents chaos, in contrast to the house which signifies a centred cosmic world. This begins to suggest the reason why Ando places so much stress on walls, why his spaces are so strongly centripetal in orientation, and why the quality and direction of light is so important.

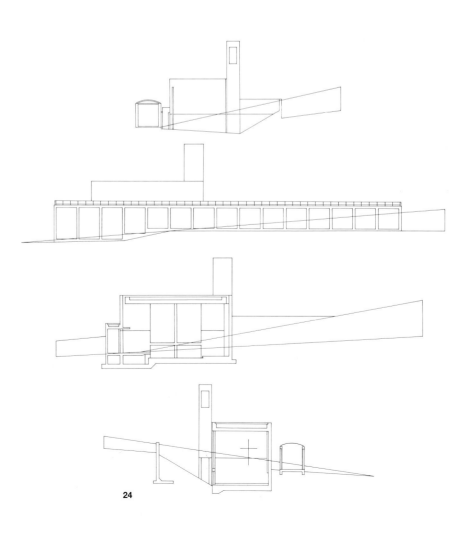

24

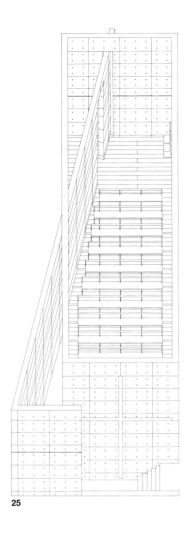

25

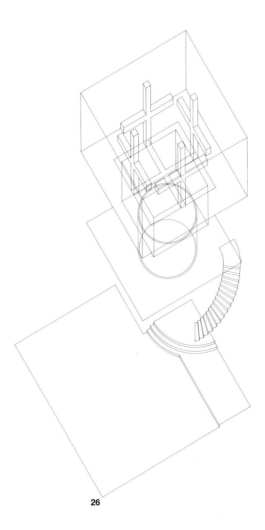

26

Space in Ando's buildings is strictly organized by means of simple geometric relationships. The Chapel on Mount Rokko, for example, is a neat square in section made up of two 6.5m cubes (6.5m wide x 13m long x 6.5m high); the Church of the Light consists of three 5.9m cubes (5.9m wide x 17.7m long x 5.9m high); while the Church on the Water is more complex, here the large 15m square space of the chapel is overlaid by a smaller 10m square on one corner which it overlaps by 5m. The pool in front consists of two 45m squares (45m wide x 90m long). The proportion of each space can be reduced to a simple ratio: 1:2:1 in the case of the Chapel on Mount Rokko, 1:3:1 for the Church of the Light, and 3 x 3 + 2 x 2 for the Church on the Water.

In drawings, the simple geometric composition of each scheme is indicated by circles.[5] These represent spheres. According to the ancient Greek philosopher Timaeus, the elements of the material world were not earth, air, fire and water, but two types of right-angled triangles. Above them were four or five solids from which all matter was constructed. The earth, we are told, was constructed of cube-shaped atoms. In order to make his architecture cosmic, Ando first chose the sphere, but since this had obvious practical difficulties he simplified it to a cube.

Where the internal space is highly geometrically organized, with integers determining the proportions of the spaces, this is at a symbolic level, paradigmatic of the cosmos. It is accompanied by a similar heightened perception of *ma* or 'nothingness'. The purpose of this is to make the individual aware of an absolute reality that transcends his being in the world. Thus, Ando's houses found the world by their geometry, by being centred, and by the use of light. The thick concrete walls keep out the chaos of the city. Why are Ando's houses designed in this way? Why must they resemble sacred space? In essence, what Ando is saying through the medium of his architecture is that humans cannot live in chaos; architecture therefore has a responsibility to create an ordered world. Ando's churches are therefore an excellent way of introducing his architecture. To create a centre is to build a world. In doing so we establish the necessary pre-conditions for dwelling.

Because the universe unfolds from the centre and stretches out towards the four

25 Church of the Light, axonometric. The volume of the building which is equivalent to three cubes, is penetrated on the long side by an L-shaped wall which exits at the back.
26 Church on the Water, axonometric. The lower, larger 15m square of the church is overlaid by a smaller 10m square on one corner, and the two are connected by a stair.
27 Ando's Naoshima Contemporary Art Museum, 1992. Chaos is interrupted by embedding geometric forms in the land.

27

29

28

30

31

cardinal points, Ando placed four crosses on top of his Church on the Water on each side of a 10 metre square. These define a centre constructed as a paradigmatic model of the world of the gods. In the Church of the Light, the cross-shaped opening at one end becomes the door to the world above, through which the gods can descend to earth and man can symbolically ascend to heaven. Allied to light, which symbolizes the divine, the austere expression of the cross as an opening in the wall makes it a kind of communion with heaven, an opening through which a symbolic passage is possible.

Homage to the wall

The importance given by Ando to walls is a distinct departure from modern architectural practice which typically downplayed the wall in the 1920s. In his 'five points' statement of 1926,[6] Le Corbusier distinguished between the structural system which carried the intermediate ceilings and rose up to the roof, and the interior walls which no longer supported the other elements of the building, and were henceforth regarded as membranes to be placed with total freedom wherever they were needed. When taken with the free design of the facade, which also lost its load-bearing role, walls could become thin elements or transparent planes. With the advent of Elementarism, walls were treated as separate vertical planes around which space flowed in a fluid and dynamic way. Mies van der Rohe's Barcelona Pavilion of 1929 was perhaps the most famous exemplar of this type of Elementarist space.

Ando's revival of the wall as a fixed containing element as well as his rejection of open universal space is contrary to Modernist architectural prejudices and also raises questions about the human significance and symbolic meaning of the wall. Indeed, his preoccupation with solid walls is close to an obsession. Ando's walls are usually made of in-situ poured concrete. They are static and permanent, and whilst considerable care is taken to see that they are as perfect as technique allows, they are massive. The main reinforced concrete shell of the Church of the Light is 380mm (15in) thick, while the external wall of the Church on the Water consists of two skins – a 250mm (10in) outer skin of concrete, 50mm

32

(2in) thickness of insulation to guard against the intense cold, and a 600mm (24in) thick inner skin, making it in total 900mm (36in) thick. A smooth surface was achieved by adopting a dense engineering quality mix with a slump less than 15cm (6in) and by ensuring thorough vibration with a minimum cover for the reinforcing bars of 5cm (2in) to avoid weathering problems and staining. The density of the concrete results in a glass-like surface that registers the different qualities of light, and this tends to dematerialize it. Because Ando's concrete is so precisely wrought, so smooth and reflective, it produces an illusion of a taut, textile surface rather than presenting itself as a heavy earthbound mass.

Ando has his own teams of expert carpenters to make the formwork who compete against each other; even so, his walls contain imperfections and are uneven. Nevertheless, his resuscitation of the wall and the return to a more traditional interpretation has important consequences.

Light is invited to play across the surface of the concrete, constantly revealing as it moves the ever-changing interdependency of light, climate and season across time.

To this end, Ando inserts vertical slots in his walls. He does the same with the roof slab, separating it from the wall with channels so that light can pour in at an incident angle in a way that reveals every minor alteration in plane, and models each curved surface in delicate chiaroscuro. Ando's walls state their thickness and density, but they also have another purpose which is to establish a human zone for the individual.

The oldest known wall found so far, in central Israel, is nearly 6,000 years old. Walls kept the weather out, but they were also a defence against other humans – they framed boundaries between territories and prevented movement. Until the eighteenth century, it was customary to build cities within a defensive wall. Indeed, a wall was a labour-saving device because it took fewer defenders to keep out an enemy.

In Homer's *Iliad*, the Achaians besieging Troy built a wall as a defence for their beached ships and for themselves.[7] The ancient Greeks employed walls as an aggressive military weapon. During the Athenian seige of Syracuse in 414BC, the Athenians ran a wall behind the Syracusan position to cut them off; no sooner had they

32 'Festival', Naha, 1984. The staccato of light from a glass block wall falling on a stair is at once abstract and modern, at the same time that it recalls the traditional shoji screen.
33 Church on the Water. The four crosses on each side of the square are joined together at their feet by a cross infilled by frosted glass blocks.
34 Church of the Light. The inwardness of the church is relieved by the splayed wall breaking through the side bringing outside light with it.

33

34

35

36

37

done this than the Syracusans retaliated by building a counter-wall.[8] Victory was decided less by strength of arms than by the extent of each army's walls. Many walls, notably Hadrian's Wall between England and Scotland, and the Great Wall of China in the Han and Ming periods, were a permanent defence against invasion. In China the ideas of 'city wall' and 'city' are closely related, as use of the same word for each, *ch'eng*, indicates.[9] The very first act in building a city was to raise a wall around it.

There are a number of things in Ando's architecture, such as his use of walls vis-à-vis the outside world to confer individuality, together with the repetition of the circle and square in his plan forms which are sugges-tive of Chinese architecture. The impor-tance attached to the wall by Ando, for one, revives traditional values which have their origin in China. There, the wall was the most essential and permanent feature of the Chinese city and its buildings, and the house, which turned a blind wall toward the street and opened to a courtyard, was the typical cell of society. The walls of Peking were an important frame that enclosed and limited the city. In fact, the whole city is a

series of large and small squares – in Chinese architecture space is conceived as a series of imbricated squares. Traditional Japanese architecture inherited the Chinese mode of closed spaces which was transplanted in the early Buddhist precincts grouped around Heijokyo in the Yamato District (Nara).

Chinese architectural space is a series of closed worlds, and is founded on geometry. In the Chinese universe the earth is con-sidered square and heaven round. These two shapes provide the basic geometrical framework for Ando's buildings. His archi-tecture is a synthesis of opposites, bringing together concepts from the East and the West. At the same time, Ando chose Josef Albers's manipulation of squares in his *Homage to the Square* series to formulate his own spaces. This arrangement of squares within squares constitutes a kind of monotonal mandala. It results, as he has explained, in '… an architecture that has been transformed from something extremely abstract and constructed according to a rigorous geometry to something representational and bearing the imprint of the human body'.[10]

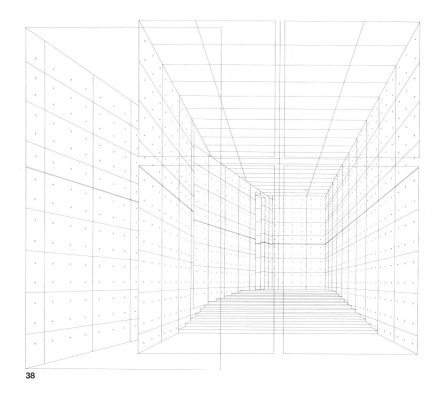
38

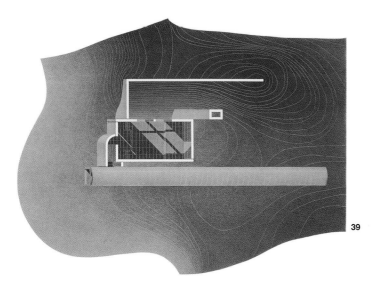

39

Inside the labyrinth

The Church on the Water is surrounded by two sets of walls. These walls establish a frame around a closed entity, but this frame is deliberately incomplete. A large L-shaped concrete wall on two sides separates the church and the pond terraces from the surrounding landscape and clearly establishes a boundary for the church precinct. The pond, which is divided into four terraces in 150mm (6in) steps, introduces yet another horizontal frame which slides underneath the building. This third frame which overlays the church is designed to connect the building with its surroundings. On the west and south it was initially contemplated that there would be a break in the strict rectangular geometry formed by a natural water edge which would remind man of the presence of nature. The idea was to have nature give a subtle nudge to the strict formal geometry of the composition. The church is a square, walled off and enclosed within a larger rectangular frame. The glazed side facing the pond can be opened completely by sliding the entire wall to one side. Ando has written: 'In the West,

a sacred space is transcendental. However, I believe that a sacred space must be related in some way to nature, which has nothing to do with animism or pantheism.'[11] By framing nature with walls, Ando seeks to geometricize it to make it more abstract. Its abstraction corresponds to man's will, and it is this which makes it sacred. The name of the church recognizes this. The church space floats above water and is further linked to it by an external cross which stands in the first water terrace.

The separation of sacred space from the chaos around it occurs to much the same extent in the Church of the Light. In this instance, however, the deployment of the walls is more involved and complex. Here, an angled wall cuts through the long west side of the main chapel at 15 degrees and exits through the end wall. This wall hooks back on itself next to the street and obscures a section of the altar elevation. Balancing this, a third low L-shaped retaining wall encloses the entry court. Walls on this occasion provide frames that isolate the sacred space from its immediate surroundings, indicating that it is a world in

39–41 The Church of the Light, Church on the Water and Chapel on Mount Rokko all repeat much the same formula of a chapel body surrounded by an outer L-shaped wall that marks out the extent of sacred space.

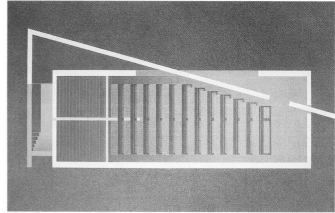

41

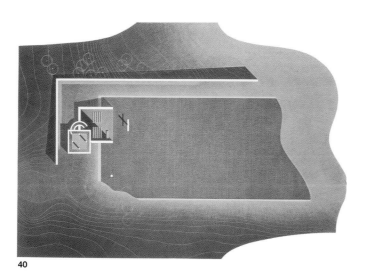

40

42 Within the enclosed, internal world of the Church of the Light, Ando has contrived to pull nature inside by drawing it through the narrow slit of the cross.
43 The chapel space at the Church on the Water has been extended by planting a large cross in the pond in front of it.
44 The labyrinthine character of the Church on the Water's composition with its surrounding wall, far from excluding nature, leads us to it by means of the water ponds.

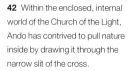

42

43

itself. The churches are detached representations of that cosmicized world rather than part of it.

In Japan, most forms of spiritual exercise take place in close proximity to nature. Normally, Ando's architecture focuses in on itself which can give it the appearance of turning its back on nature. His aim is to create spaces that are alive, that are single shells on the outside and labyrinthine inside, into which nature is drawn. Walls are agents of this internal world. The forms used in the architecture are simplified to the point where we are tempted to forget them altogether. The internal spaces behave as complex sundials aided by such contrivances as skylights, slits and curved walls, which, when seen from the inside, give the impression of being buried in the earth. In this respect, light, not the solid concrete walls, is the principal goal of the architecture.

In both churches Ando took on the challenge of bringing nature *inside*. He wanted man and nature to confront each other within the enclosed, internal world of his architecture. This involved creating a tension between the two which is expressly resolved in the 'nothingness' of the internal

space. To achieve this Ando conceived his buildings almost as land art, buried places that struggle to emerge from the earth, which, by their struggle, dramatize the encounter between architecture and nature.

The cross is the leading symbol in both works. The Church of the Light is a functioning Christian church on the outskirts of Osaka that serves the local Ibaraki community. The Church on the Water is a Western-style wedding chapel for honeymooning couples at the northern Tomamu resort on Hokkaido.

In order to draw nature inside, Ando found it necessary to lead his architecture to nature; the large pond in front of the Church on the Water links the two. The external cross outside the building in the water extends the symbol beyond the architectural frame. The cross cut out in the concrete wall at the front of the Church of the Light is a variation of this same idea. Looking at the cross one sees beyond it in one's imagination, while, because the interior is so contained the space tends to implode. It is as if the pressure inside falls and air swirls in through the open cross from the outside.

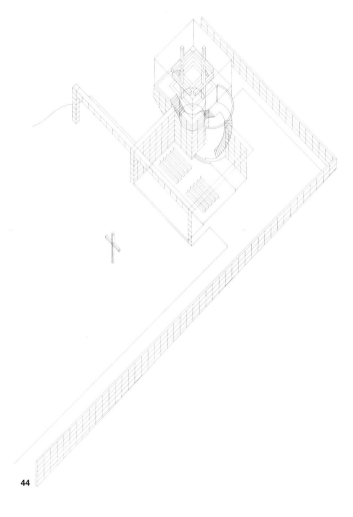

44

45

The four crosses mounted inside the glazed cube above the Church on the Water offer a three-dimensional version of this phenomenon. The transparent wall around the crosses is a reminder to us of the form from which the four crosses were carved. This powerful gesture sets one's minds to work mentally reconstructing the original cube. Standing inside at the centre and looking out between the crosses, the viewer is surrounded by four figures which frame the landscape of the surrounding hills and woods.

This use of the cross as a symbolic form in the landscape has a long history in Europe and there are corresponding gestures in traditional Japanese architecture. The *torii* in the bay at the Itsukishima shrine on the island of Miyajima beside the Inland Sea is a most impressive example of the projection of a frame in nature which simultaneously pulls the bay into the shrine.

In Europe, crucifixes were frequently erected in Catholic countries as a memorial or an object of pilgrimage in the landscape. In his paintings *The Cross in the Mountains*, 1807–08, and *Morning in the Riesengebirge*,

1810–11, Caspar David Friedrich depicted this type of crucifix. In the former image, the cross is on a hill-top with the figure of Christ on the crucifix facing the dying light of the setting sun. *The Cross in the Mountains* expresses a sentiment of transcendental pantheism, while in *Morning in the Riesengebirge*, the crucifix appears in the clear light of sunrise in a serene windless landscape from which all turbulence and disturbance has been removed. Here, the purity of the light and infinity of the horizon bring God closer.

The architectural elaboration of this motif makes its appearance in the Woodland Crematorium at Sockenvagen outside Stockholm, 1940, by Gunnar Asplund, and later in the Chapel of the Technical University at Otaniemi, 1957, by Kaija and Heikki Siren. This latter example is the direct precursor of Ando's Church on the Water. In Gunnar Asplund's Forest Crematorium, a monumental cross was erected on rising ground some distance beyond the portico of the main chapel. Mourners glimpsed it on their way to the crematorium. Asplund introduced an influential innovation in a bronze and glass

45 The appearance of the cross in the landscape has a long history in Europe which has parallels in Japanese architecture.
46 The *torii* in the bay at Miyajima marks the gateway in the seaward procession towards the temple shrine, but seen from the temple building, extends it out into the bay.
47 Caspar David Friedrich gave Christ's crucifixion a specifically northern context and relevance, here shown in a detail of the painting *Morning in the Riesengebirge*, 1810–11.
48 Friedrich's *The Cross in the Mountains*, 1907–08, expresses a transcendental pantheism merging into nature.

47

48

46

50

49

49 With the glass wall slid to one side, the chapel becomes a veranda-like space concentrating our attention on the primary focus – the crucifix in the pond.
50 All five faces of the upper cube have crosses; only the top is left open to accept the vertical sacred axis.
51 The Technical University Chapel by Kaija and Heiki Siren, Otaniemi, 1957: relocating the cross outside and placing it in a forest clearing changes our whole perception of this space.
52 At Gunnar Asplund's Woodland Crematorium, Stockholm, 1940, the cross is employed as a sign in the landscape, introducing the crematorium chapel seen beyond in the distance – the very opposite of the Siren's building.

51

52

door of the church which can be lowered into the ground to unify the space of the building and the court. Hence, the Church on the Water incorporates ideas from both buildings in its use of the external cross framed by the forest trees and the removable wall.

However, it was the Siren's Otaniemi Chapel that had the greatest influence on Ando. The placement of the cross outside the church beyond the altar is the one thing that contributed most to increasing the identification of the building with its environment. It leads, as in the Caspar David Friedrich paintings, to a pantheistic religious expression in which nature is made the primary focus of the chapel which assumes a dependent status as a shelter joined to, and serving, the cross in its beautiful setting. The stained timber screen-wall around the entry forecourt was repeated in the Church of the Light. Here, an L-shaped concrete wall leads worshippers around the church to the entrance.

In following the Siren's precedent, Ando did not necessarily accept its pantheistic premise of god in nature so much as reinforce the traditional Japanese idea that all forms of spiritual exercise benefit from contact with nature. This affinity between Finnish and Japanese attitudes towards nature is also revealed in some of the early works of Alvar Aalto.

Ando's buildings force people to confront nature. This produces a kind of electrical charge between architecture and nature; depending on how you choose to read it, it either leads us out into the landscape, or draws nature inside. Either way, nature and architecture form a duality which Ando holds in tension as a simple opposition. In both the Church of the Light and Church on the Water, this duality is brought to the fore as a focus of religious feeling by freeing the chief symbol, the cross, and removing it to the outside so that it is included in nature, but still functions as the essential and central sign of the architecture. Removing the cross from the interior of each church, far from diminishing its power, actually increases its impact.

Light and darkness
The Church of the Light is a rather small building, hidden by pine trees, on the corner of two streets at Ibaraki. It is located 25km north–northeast of Osaka in the western

foothills of the Yodo valley railway corridor linking Osaka with Kyoto. The residential streets around it are quite narrow. The church itself is comparatively small having an area of 113sq m (1216 sq ft) – about the same size as a small house.

The building took more than two years to complete. It is used for classical concerts and community meetings as well as holding Christian services. The delay in completing the work was due to problems in raising the necessary funds. Initially it was feared that it would cost more than the budget and Ando even considered building it without a roof, but the construction firm donated the roof and this move became unnecessary.

Access to the church is intentionally indirect. Worshippers are required to enter the site at the northeast corner off a side street via a forecourt which leads around a corner of the church to the minister's house. From here, the route about turns and skips forward in a convoluted 'S' movement that takes the visitor through an opening in the long wall of the church and leads on to a second 1.60m wide by 5.35m high doorway in the angled blade wall. This is disorienting and creates a feeling of apprehension and

heightened expectation about what will follow next. One is soon rewarded by the wholly unexpected impact of the cross of light filling the surrounding darkness at the opposite end of the church.

The difficult entry serves to emphasize the movement across the threshold from the outside into the sacred interior. It has a similar effect to the 'kneeling in' entrance of the tea house which was intended to inculcate humility in all who enter. Ando's attitude to materials is also similar. In the tea house materials are plain and undecorated, colour and texture resulting directly from the nature of the materials used. As in the tea house, there are few openings inside the church, and these, with the exception of the cross opening at the front, admit a soft, diffused light. The floors and seats are made from rough timber planks of reclaimed scaffolding boards – this lowered the cost substantially. The choice of a natural material such as timber for the seating also relieves the coldness of the concrete and lends an overall feeling of warmth to the interior. Ando prefers to use natural materials where they come in contact with people because they are so tactile.

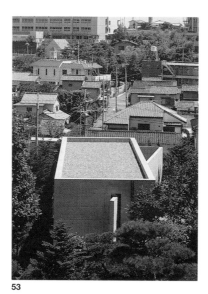

53

54

55

53 The Church of the Light is relatively small, hemmed in by housing. Its simple shoe-box like form is punctured by a single wall angled at 15 degrees which re-emerges at the back.
54 In a surprising reversal of Christian customs, the floor of the church steps down towards the altar; this lifts the congregation up in relation to the dominance of the cross-opening in the wall.
55 A screen of pine trees on two sides shields the building and acts as a foil to the brutal simplicity of its cubic form.

57

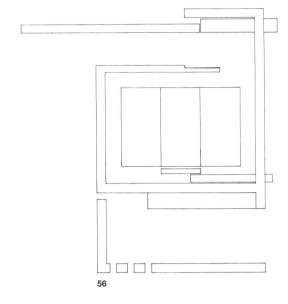

56

58

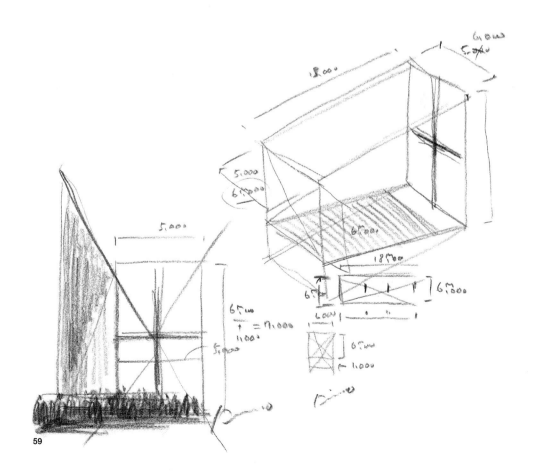

59

56 The church's arrangement repeats the basic composition of the concrete tea house of the Yamaguchi House, 1982, with its cubic body penetrated by a free-standing L-shaped wall.
57 Abbey at Sénanque, Provence. On the outside, this twelfth-century Cistercian abbey consists of two intersecting walls which are concentrated where their axes intersect.
58 The effect of the plain tunnel-vaulted interior of the Abbey at Sénanque depends almost entirely on the effect of light.
59 Ando's sketches clearly demonstrate his aesthetic idea which was a telescoping volume expanding towards the cross and lifting so as to indicate the point where the vertical and horizontal lines intersect in the cross.

Once inside, the eye takes time to adjust to the gloom. Besides the cross punched out of the front wall, which in any case is only 20cm wide, a second full-height glazed opening is provided towards the rear where the diagonal blade of concrete slices through the side of the building. This helps to soften the contrast between the brilliant light of the cross and the darkened interior. The cross opening in the end wall is the principal daylight source, although this is supplemented by four small light fittings on the opposite wall. Light is reflected off the ceiling and walls by the glass-like concrete which helps to distribute the light more evenly.

Despite its traditional eastern end and radiant light, the form as a whole stems as much from the concrete tea house which Ando added in 1982 to his Yamaguchi House at Takarazuka, Hyogo, 1974–82, as it does from the more familiar model of the Western basilica. Ando has written that it was inspired by the Abbey at Sénanque in Provence which he visited in the 1960s.[12] The mixture of Eastern and Western motifs is fairly typical – Ando often deploys oriental and Japanese types with countervailing Western paradigms. It arises from his goal of fusing opposite spatial concepts into a fluid transcendental architecture. This is also about the integration of two opposites, abstraction and representation. (Moreover Ando himself is a twin which might help to explain his fascination with pairs of ideas.)

Early designs for the church showed the floor plan with pews in the middle and side access, which has not in fact been followed in practice. The church is split down the middle by a central aisle in line with the cross. The rows of seats are arranged on ten 10cm high by 90cm deep stained board terraces and the floor descends towards the altar. The cross opening symbolizes the intention of extreme economy imposed by the small budget.

The windows employ the same grey metal section used throughout Ando's work. For the cross, the 16mm float glass is fixed in the concrete without a frame to heighten further the dramatic effect of the light streaming through it. A horizontal groove, 3.95m above the floor, runs around the walls both inside and outside to coincide with the height of the underside of the cross transom. An 18cm high gap has been left below the ceiling and the top of the angled blade wall. This separates it from the body of the church and expresses it as an autonomous and distinct element of the architecture.

Because it is so introspective and closed, the interior is strongly focused on the cross of light. The minister stands at a lectern on the right hand side from where he gives the lesson and directs the service. He preaches from below rather than from the more conventional elevated position above the congregation; it took Ando some time to persuade the minister and congregation on this point.

Water and sky

The Church on the Water is a much larger work. It is exactly three times the size of the Church of the Light with an area of 345sq m, and was designed well before it in mid-1985. Work did not commence until early 1988, but when it did it progressed very rapidly. The Church on the Water is located at Tomamu on a plain northeast of the Yubari Mountains which lie to the east of Sapporo on the northern island of Hokkaido.

The church is sited in a large clearing in a forest of beech trees on a sloping site that falls gently towards the nearby river. A low hill with a chair lift to the west dominates the prospect. A resort hotel complex is located behind the church to the east. Approximately 400 metres away northwest of the Church on the Water, an open amphitheatre is planned, although this building has not yet been realized. This facility has an anticipated capacity of about 6,000 seated in a semi-circular shaped bowl overlooking a fan-shaped artificial lake. It was intended for concerts in the warmer spring and summer seasons, while in winter the lake will become a skating rink. The Tomamu region is covered with snow from December to April when it is transformed into a beautiful white expanse.

Ando linked the two facilities, first, by a wall that points towards the church, and second, by the river lower down which bounds the large pond along its western edge. Water is diverted from this river into the 80m x 42.7m pond. The Church on the Water is set at the opposite east bank at one end of the pond on high ground.

60

60 This sketch shows a somewhat different conception – the two overlapping squares are there, as is the pond, and including the outside wall, but the overlapping motif is repeated on the right leading into the pond.
61 The site of the chapel falls gently towards the nearby river seen in the foreground. Behind it lies the resort hotel complex.

61

62 The long wall along the two sides of the Church on the Water hides the pond until the visitor reaches the entrance; at the same time, it wrestles the sacred from the mundane much as in a Buddhist temple complex.

63 The church is based on two overlapping squares, the larger lower chapel 15m x 15m surmounted by a smaller square 10m x 10m.

62

The building consists of two squares, one 10 metres square and another 15 metres square; the two overlap in plan at one corner and are aligned along the same longitudinal axis as the pond. This asymmetrical group is framed by a 39.45m x 75.425m long freestanding L-shaped concrete wall on the east and south which serves to isolate the church from the hotel behind it.

The wall obscures the pond terraces which are glimpsed only after the visitor has rounded the wall at its extreme northernmost point. The rectangular water terrace is framed at this point by the 6.2m high flying beam-and-column wing used to support the glass wall which extends 15.9m out from the church. A modest entry is provided in the base of the glass cube through a doorway in the exposed concrete, and a deliberately circuitous approach takes the visitor down outside the L-shaped wall on the south and back up to the rear of the chapel. From here, the visitor is led up over and around four crosses which face one another across a square transparent glass roof made up of 16 panels of 15mm thick laminated float glass supported on

250mm deep H-section steel beams above the waiting-room level at the rear of the building. The circular-shaped lobby below it has a second glass ceiling in 6mm thick float glass.

The cube of light, with four crosses inside it, is connected to the main chapel by a dark semi-circular concrete stairway which protrudes from the back wall of the church in a cylindrical bulge. The 15mm float glass screen surrounding the crosses lifts the eye towards the sky framing it as it does so. Within this glass cube, the visitor is enveloped in light. The glare from the main window-wall was counterbalanced in the Siren's Chapel at Otaniemi by a large window behind and above the congregation. At Tomamu, the glass cube has replaced the rear window, but it no longer assists in reducing the glare of the window-wall at the front of the church. It becomes just another element in a dramatic sequence of controlled 'light experiences', as one passes from the brilliant light of the open sky on the exposed platform with its four crucifixes, to the darkened confined stairway leading down into the church, and thence, into the protected cave of

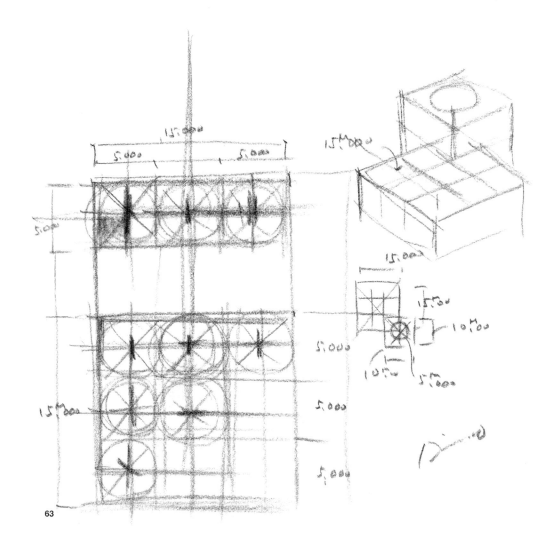

63

64

the chapel. Its open front looks directly out across the horizontal expanse of the water which in turn bounces light into the interior space where it is trapped.

As has already been noted, the glazed wall facing the pond slides open, exposing the interior to the outside and thereby producing an entirely new sense of intimacy with the church's surroundings. The heavy glass wall travels on an I-section steel track housed inside a massive inverted U-shaped steel structural beam. The marriage celebrants can feel they are outside while at the same time they are protected by a roof. The space, like a cave or gallery, parcels off a small fragment of universal space that is more in keeping with the human dimension. Opening up the church in this way creates an ambiguity which is much like that experienced inside a veranda, raising a sudden doubt as to the certainty of inside and the distinctness of outside.

The transparent cube of the four crosses draws the sacred vertical axis down to earth and spins it around so it darts from the building out into the landscape. The lower level, with its facilities for dressing, serves as a transitional lock. The four crosses are

50cm square in concrete and stand in a 6.5m square which is divided symmetrically into four 2.5m smaller glazed squares. The walkway, which consists of two up and two down stairs, circumambulates this quadrille of crucifixes. There is a stairway on each side, two up and two down, leading up from the entry then back down to the circular stair access to the chapel. The glass wall surrounding the crosses is supported by an H-section steel frame on the inside, and C-sections on the outside; all the steelwork is rustproofed and coated with fluorine resin. The glass screen is made of 15mm thick float glass. Directly under this is a translucent cylindrical-shaped glass antechamber with sliding doors giving access to three waiting rooms and male and female lavatories arranged around a cylindrical glass lobby.

The main chapel is relatively uncluttered. There are five rows of brown-stained timber bench seats in pairs on either side of the centre aisle. These are simply made up of horizontal and vertical members. The arm- and back-rests are subtly curved in a manner that invites the hand to touch them. The rear of the church on one side is taken

64 The framing effect of the building is increased at night by illuminating the cross and the adjoining beech forest.
65 Its abstract geometry utilizes the impact of single-point per-spective where every line is made to converge on the centre of the cross.

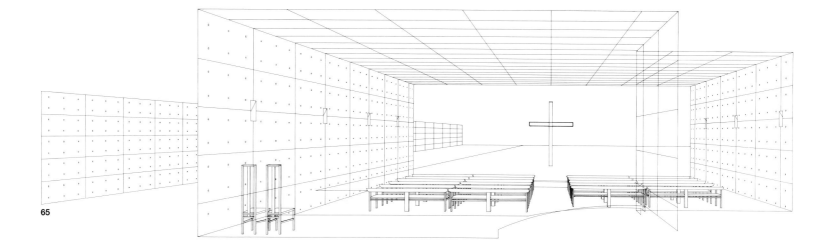

65

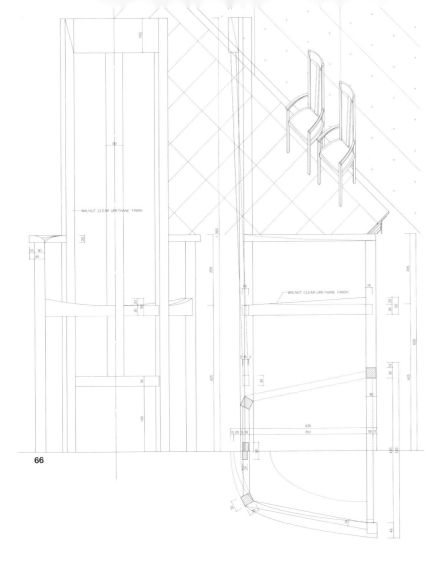

66

67

66, 67 Two chairs designed by
Ando have been placed at the
rear of the church.
68 In its two aspects, the building succeeds in bringing the vertical sacred axis at the back into
collision with the horizontal earth
axis entering from the front.

up by the dressing area which overlaps the chapel and from which issue three circular steps which press forward into the main space. With the exception of two Ando-designed chairs at the back, the opposite side is empty. The floor is covered in black granite slabs.

Bringing the divine to life

Ando has written: 'I want to give nature's power a presence in contemporary society and provide thereby the kind of stimulating places that speak directly to man's every sense as a living, corporeal being. More-over, retrieving from history's strata not form or style but the essential view of nature and life that runs through its depths – the spirit of culture, in other words.'[12]

What role do these churches serve? What is the function of the sacred in this? The sacred reveals to us what it means to be good and challenges us to be better human beings. It introduces the spiritual rising up out of life and gives it a heightened signi-ficance by its gesture of setting aside a special realm. In these two works by Tadao Ando ordinary materials are ennobled and given new meaning in ways that we least

expect; he introduces the temporal dimension of sunlight and so makes us more aware of things through his disposition of walls and openings. Thus we are sensitized to nature, to shadows and the wind, to the sounds around us, to what it means to be fully alive to where we are.

By harnessing geometry, Ando centres people and creates the perfect circumstances for people to dwell in the world. The sacred is present in all his work to some extent; in these buildings only more so. The Church of the Light and Church on the Water complement each other. Two countervailing ideas are juxtaposed in the crucifix and the empty silence of the void as a sign of 'nothingness' – the sign of the West against the non-sign of the East. In the Church of the Light, the cross is a void drawing God inside its emptiness; in the Church on the Water, this is reversed – four solid crosses facing out in the four universal axes that orientate us. One is simple, but complex in its simplicity, the other is complex, yet simple in its complexity. They are constructed from within like a tea house. That is their special secret.

68

Church of the Light (right)
Entry to the building from the
narrow side street is indirect and
far from obvious.

Church on the Water (far right)
View from lowest water pond
with the freestanding beam
housing the track for the horizontal sliding wall visible to one
side of the church behind the
external cross.

Church on the Water

View from the northeast corner over the building to a low hill on the west. Below the church is a small river which defines the southern boundary of the water ponds.

Church on the Water
(left) Side elevation of the building behind the outer enclosing wall which returns across the hillside. The entrance to the church is partly visible below the upper cube frame containing the four crosses.
(right) Only when past the end of the wall is the entrance fully visible in the concrete base.

Church on the Water
(left) Detail of the top of the
concrete base and stair wall
with the cubic space frame
above it.
(right) Entrance to the church is
at the rear with stairs leading
onto the top of the smaller upper
cube of crosses.

Church on the Water
(left and above) Below the four crosses is a cylindrical-shaped antechamber with alcoves; waiting rooms and lavatories are located around it. The photograph above shows the underside of the translucent glass roof. (right) Above the vestibule two pairs of concrete crosses confront each other within a steel cubic frame.

Church on the Water
(far left) The displacement of the steel cross in front of the open interior in the first of the ponds draws the space out into the landscape.
(left) A semi-circular stair leads down from the entrance to the rear of the church.
(above and right) There are five rows of pews of brown-stained timber on either side of the central aisle.

Church on the Water
(below) The beam carrying the
sliding track for the glass wall
also doubles as a frame for this
view of the ponds. The cross can
be seen on the far left.
(right) Side view across the
upper pond in front of the
church.

Church on the Water
(above) The church seen
shrouded in snow in the winter,
with the glass sliding wall behind
the cross closed.
(right) View from the south
below the church shows the
side extension of the facade to
accommodate the horizontal
sliding glass wall, with the
smaller upper cube containing
the freestanding concrete
crosses above it on the left.

Church of the Light

(right) Rooftop view: the building
is hidden by foliage and the
roofs of nearby houses.
(far right) The end wall with its
cross-opening is framed by a
screen of trees between it and
the street.

Church of the Light
(left) Inside, behind the end wall, light flooding through the narrow cross aperture is reflected on the smooth concrete walls and ceiling.
(right) View across the church towards the front from the entrance on the right in the splay-wall.

Church of the Light
(left) View of the entrance in the splay-wall as it penetrates the rear of the church through an opening.
(right) Pews on the right side beside the opening; the splay-wall slides past into the church space.

Church of the Light
(far left) Detail of the window and
splay-wall at the line where it
breaks through the wall plane.
A gap has been left below
the ceiling and the top of the
splay-wall.
(left, above and right) Light
seeps through the narrow slots
in the walls and is reflected by
the smooth concrete which has
a glass-like finish.

Church of the Light

The cross motif is repeated in the ends of the timber pews and is caught by beams of light as it crosses the floor, evoking an austere atmosphere, yet calm at the same time.

Church on the Water

Drawings

Site plan

(Ando's proposed Theatre on
the Water is shown to the north
of the church)

| 0 | 50m |
| 0 | 150ft |

Elevation

Section

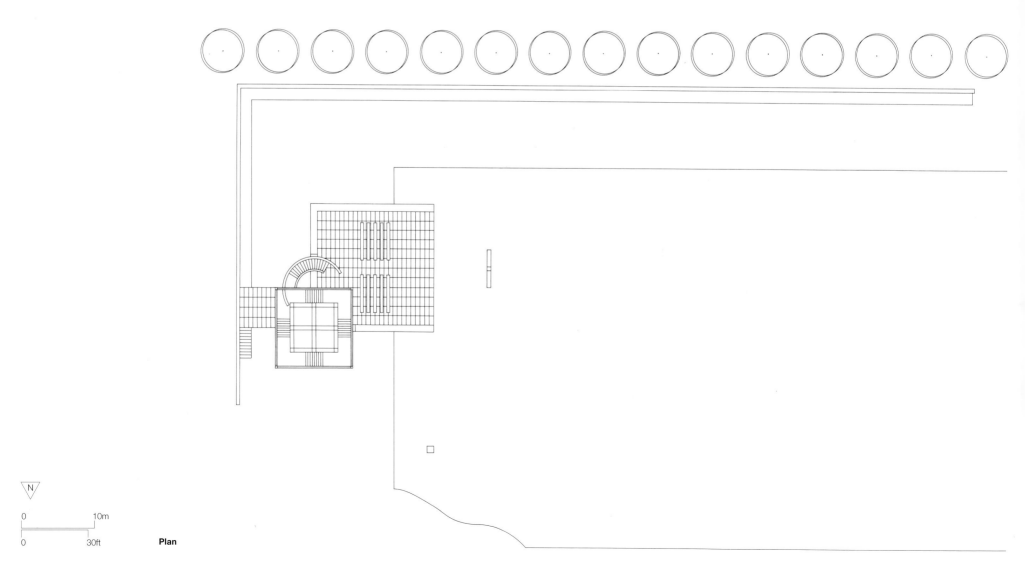

N

0   10m

0   30ft

Plan

**First floor plan and
details of movable screen**

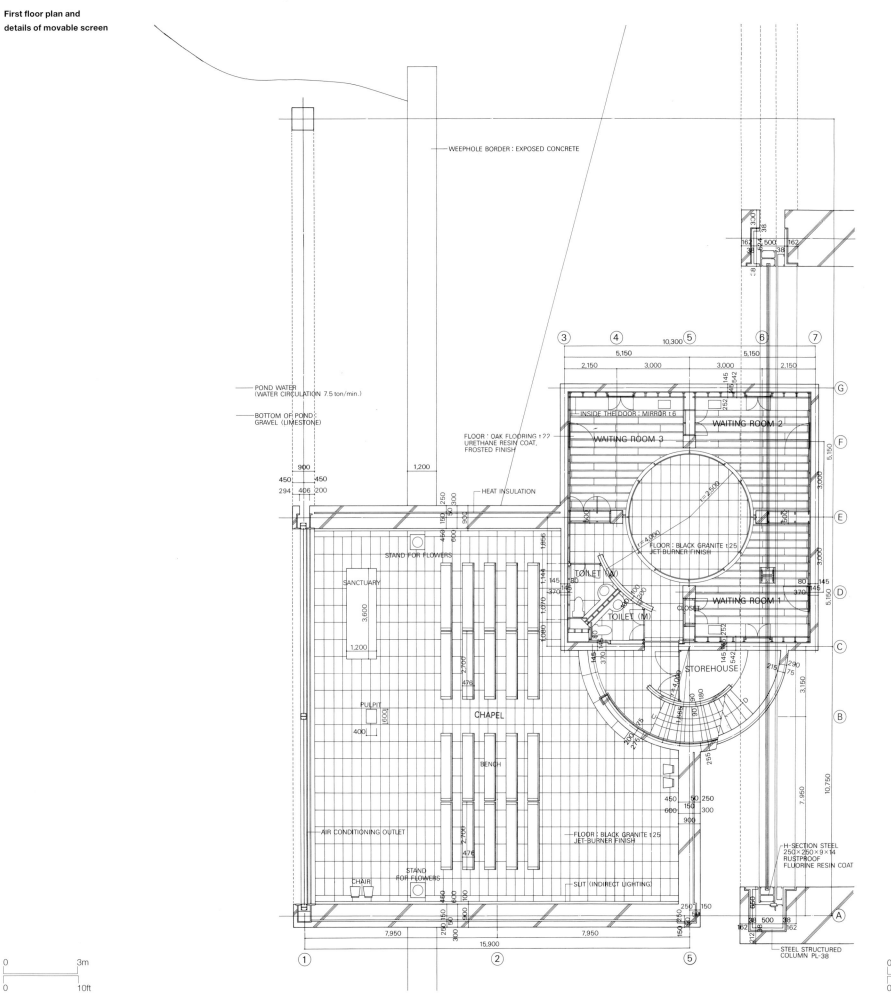

WEEPHOLE BORDER : EXPOSED CONCRETE

POND WATER
(WATER CIRCULATION 7.5 ton/min.)

BOTTOM OF POND
GRAVEL (LIMESTONE)

FLOOR : OAK FLOORING t22
URETHANE RESIN COAT,
FROSTED FINISH

HEAT INSULATION

INSIDE THE DOOR : MIRROR t6

WAITING ROOM 3

WAITING ROOM 2

FLOOR : BLACK GRANITE t25
JET-BURNER FINISH

STAND FOR FLOWERS

SANCTUARY

TOILET (W)

TOILET (M)

WAITING ROOM 1

CLOSET

PULPIT

STOREHOUSE

CHAPEL

BENCH

AIR CONDITIONING OUTLET

FLOOR : BLACK GRANITE t25
JET-BURNER FINISH

H-SECTION STEEL
250×250×9×14
RUSTPROOF
FLUORINE RESIN COAT

CHAIR

STAND
FOR FLOWERS

SLIT (INDIRECT LIGHTING)

STEEL STRUCTURED
COLUMN PL-38

0   3m

0   10ft

0   1m

0   3ft

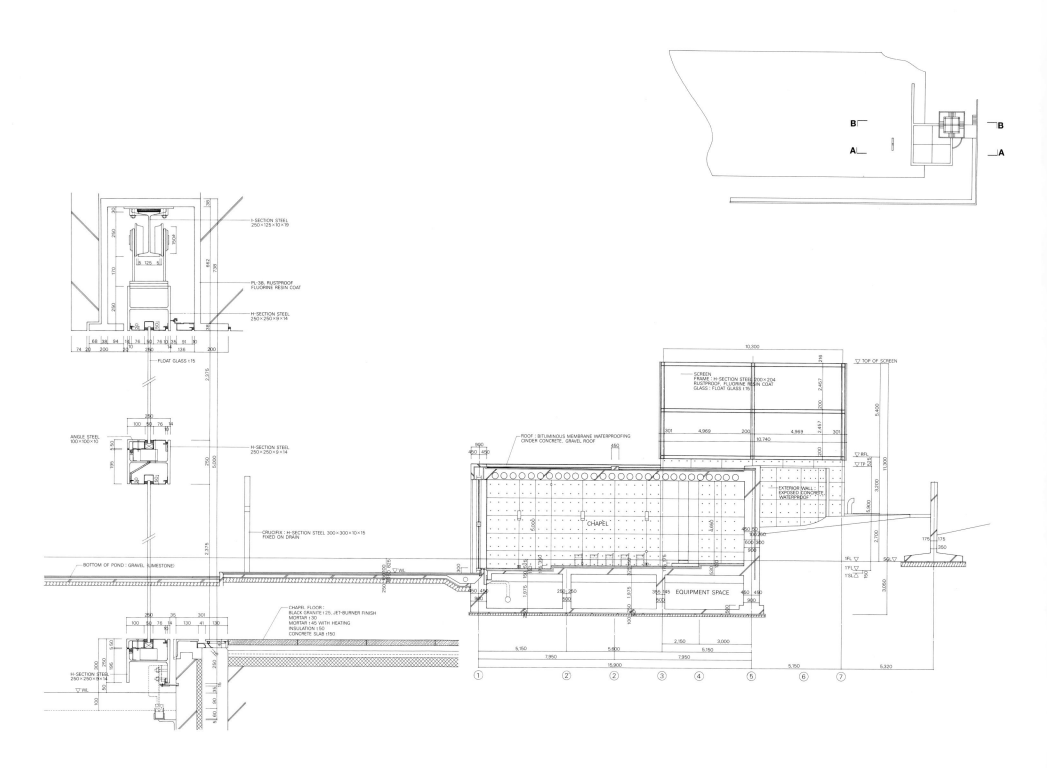

I-SECTION STEEL
250×125×10×19

PL-38. RUSTPROOF
FLUORINE RESIN COAT

H-SECTION STEEL
250×250×9×14

FLOAT GLASS t 15

ANGLE STEEL
100×100×10

H-SECTION STEEL
250×250×9×14

CRUCIFIX : H-SECTION STEEL 300×300×10×15
FIXED ON DRAIN

BOTTOM OF POND : GRAVEL (LIMESTONE)

CHAPEL FLOOR :
BLACK GRANITE t 25, JET-BURNER FINISH
MORTAR t 30
MORTAR t 45 WITH HEATING
INSULATION t 50
CONCRETE SLAB t 150

H-SECTION STEEL
250×250×9×14

SCREEN
FRAME : H-SECTION STEEL 200×204
RUSTPROOF, FLUORINE RESIN COAT
GLASS : FLOAT GLASS t 15

ROOF : BITUMINOUS MEMBRANE WATERPROOFING
CINDER CONCRETE, GRAVEL ROOF

EXTERIOR WALL :
EXPOSED CONCRETE
WATERPROOF

CHAPEL

EQUIPMENT SPACE

**Perspective of church and
details of movable screen**

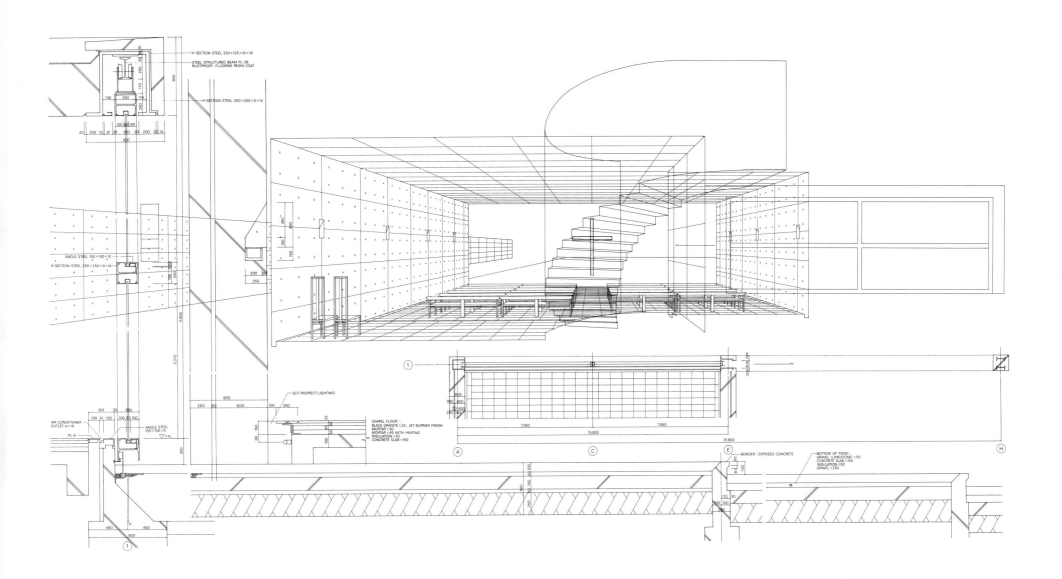

H-SECTION STEEL 250×125×10×19

STEEL STRUCTURED BEAM PL-38
RUSTPROOF, FLUORINE RESIN COAT

H-SECTION STEEL 250×250×9×14

ANGLE STEEL 100×100×10

H-SECTION STEEL 250×250×9×14

AIR CONDITIONER
OUTLET w=41

ANGLE STEEL
150×100×9

SLIT (INDIRECT/LIGHTING)

CHAPEL FLOOR :
BLACK GRANITE : 25, JET-BURNER FINISH
MORTAR : 30
MORTAR : 45 WITH HEATING
INSULATION : 50
CONCRETE SLAB : 150

BORDER : EXPOSED CONCRETE

BOTTOM OF POND :
GRAVEL (LIMESTONE) : 150
CONCRETE SLAB : 150
INSULATION : 50
GRAVEL : 250

0   500mm

0   18in

**Section BB, axonometric and
details of roof and glass screen**

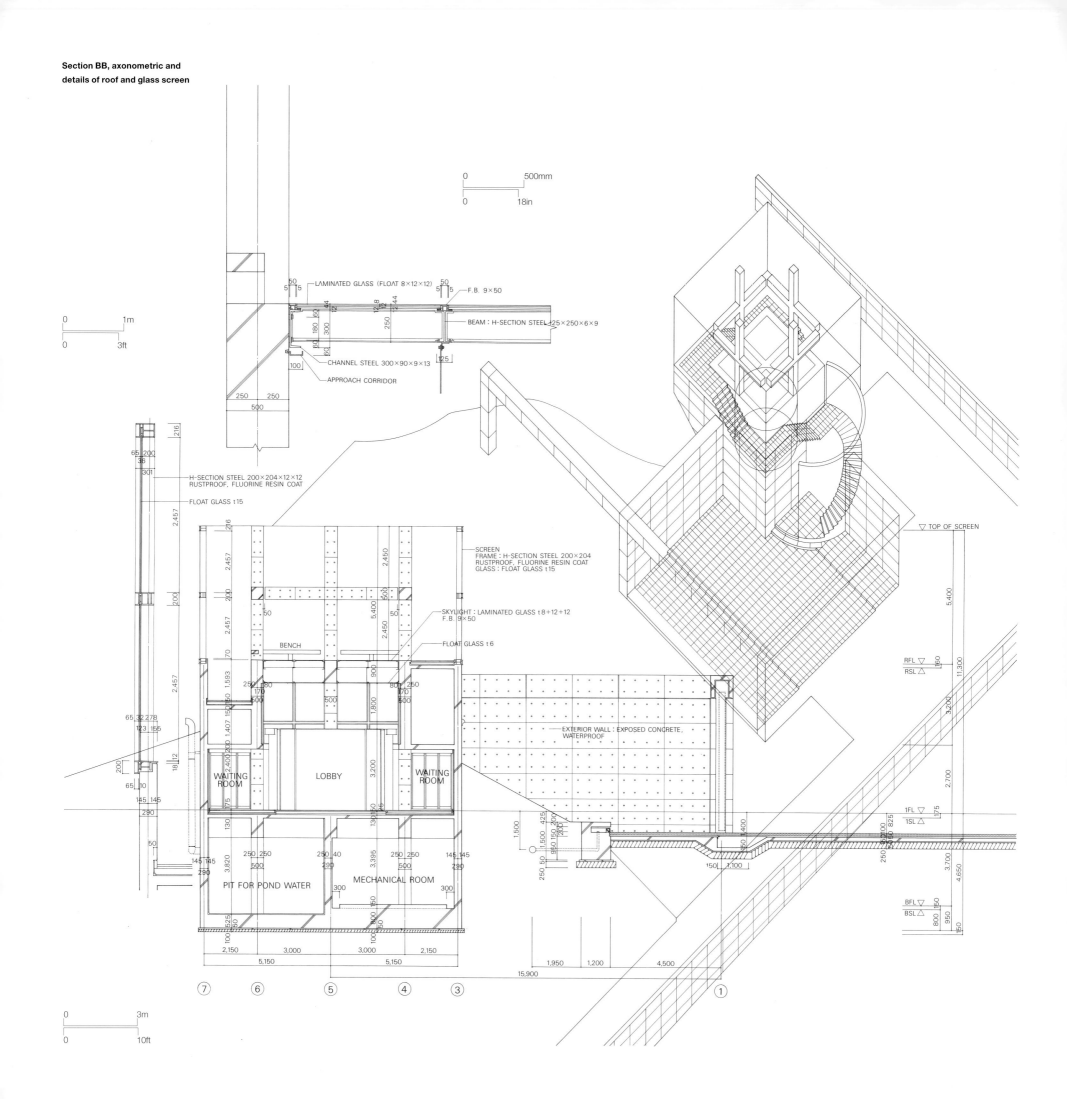

0 ____ 500mm
0 ____ 18in

0 ____ 1m
0 ____ 3ft

50
5 5 LAMINATED GLASS (FLOAT 8×12×12) 50
5 5   F.B. 9×50

BEAM : H-SECTION STEEL 125×250×6×9

CHANNEL STEEL 300×90×9×13

APPROACH CORRIDOR

250 250
500

216
65 200
36
301   H-SECTION STEEL 200×204×12×12
RUSTPROOF, FLUORINE RESIN COAT

FLOAT GLASS t15

2.457

216

2.457

2.450

2.450

5.400

500

500

200

200

2.457

2.457

SCREEN
FRAME : H-SECTION STEEL 200×204
RUSTPROOF, FLUORINE RESIN COAT
GLASS : FLOAT GLASS t15

SKYLIGHT : LAMINATED GLASS t 8+12+12
F.B. 9×50

FLOAT GLASS t 6

BENCH

900

250 180   800 250
170   170
500   500

1.593
250
1.800   1.800

65 32 278
123 155

2.457

200
18 12

EXTERIOR WALL : EXPOSED CONCRETE,
WATERPROOF

1.407
200 150

2.400

65 10

145 145
290

WAITING
ROOM

LOBBY

3.200

WAITING
ROOM

3.200

130   130

TOP OF SCREEN

RFL ▽   150
RSL △

5.400

11.300

3.200

2.700

50

145 145
290

3.820

PIT FOR POND WATER

250 250   250 40
290

500

3.395

MECHANICAL ROOM

300

250 250   145 145
500   290

300

1.500

1.500 150 200
950

425
200

1FL ▽   175
1SL △

250
825

150

150 1.100

4.650

3.700

BFL ▽ 150
BSL △

800 950

150

525
100 50

2,150   3,000   3,000   2,150
5,150   5,150

⑦   ⑥   ⑤   ④   ③

1,950 1,200   4,500
15,900

①

0 ____ 3m
0 ____ 10ft

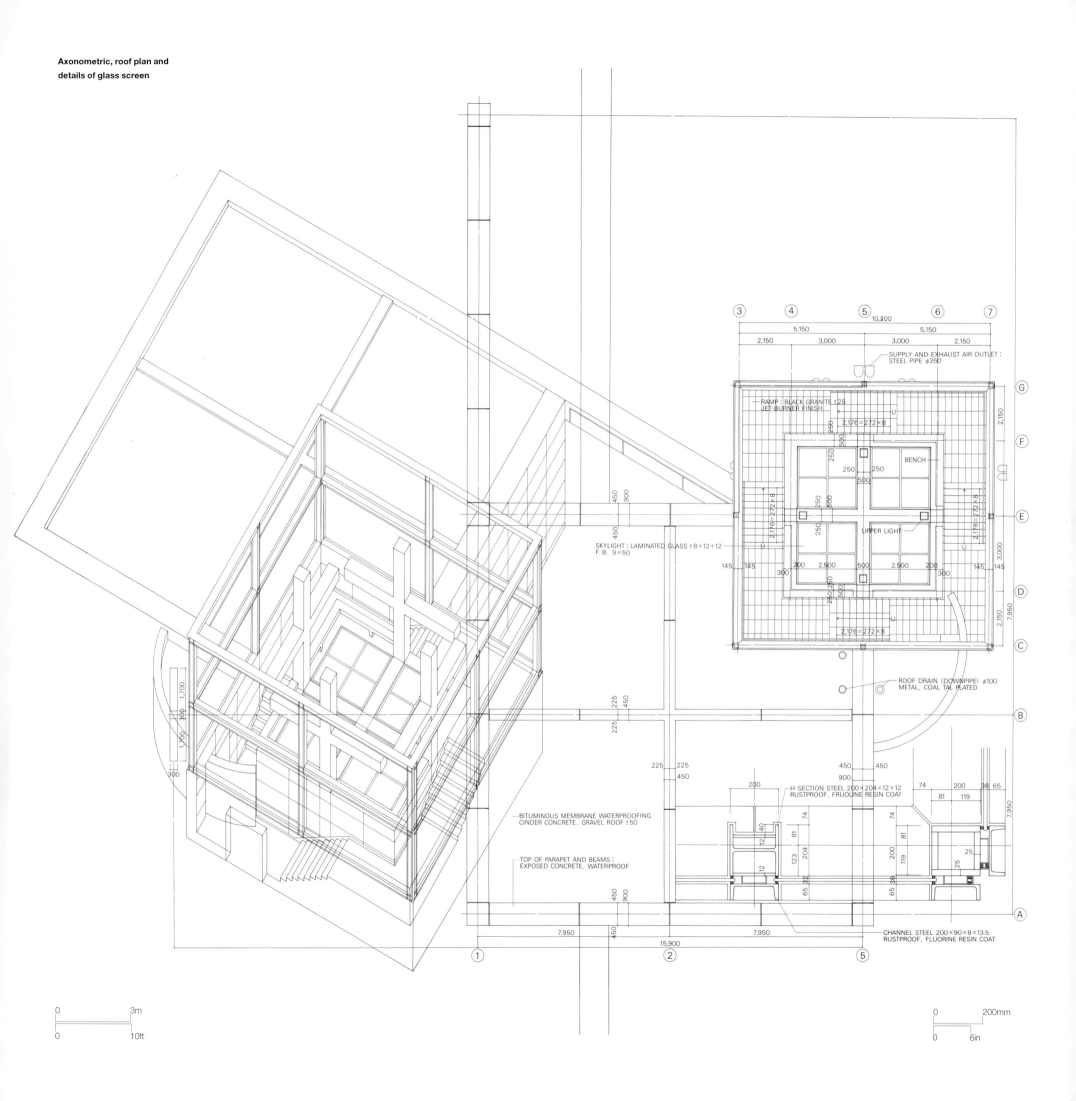

SUPPLY AND EXHAUST AIR OUTLET :
STEEL PIPE φ350

RAMP : BLACK GRANITE t 25
JET-BURNER FINISH

2,176=272×8

BENCH

UPPER LIGHT

2,176=272×8

SKYLIGHT : LAMINATED GLASS t 8+12+12
F. B. 9×50

2,176=272×8

ROOF DRAIN (DOWNPIPE) φ100
METAL. COAL TAL PLATED

H-SECTION STEEL 200×204×12×12
RUSTPROOF, FRUOLINE RESIN COAT

BITUMINOUS MEMBRANE WATERPROOFING
CINDER CONCRETE, GRAVEL ROOF t 50

TOP OF PARAPET AND BEAMS :
EXPOSED CONCRETE, WATERPROOF

CHANNEL STEEL 200×90×8×13.5
RUSTPROOF, FLUORINE RESIN COAT

0   3m

0   10ft

0   200mm

0   6in

Church of the Light

Site plan

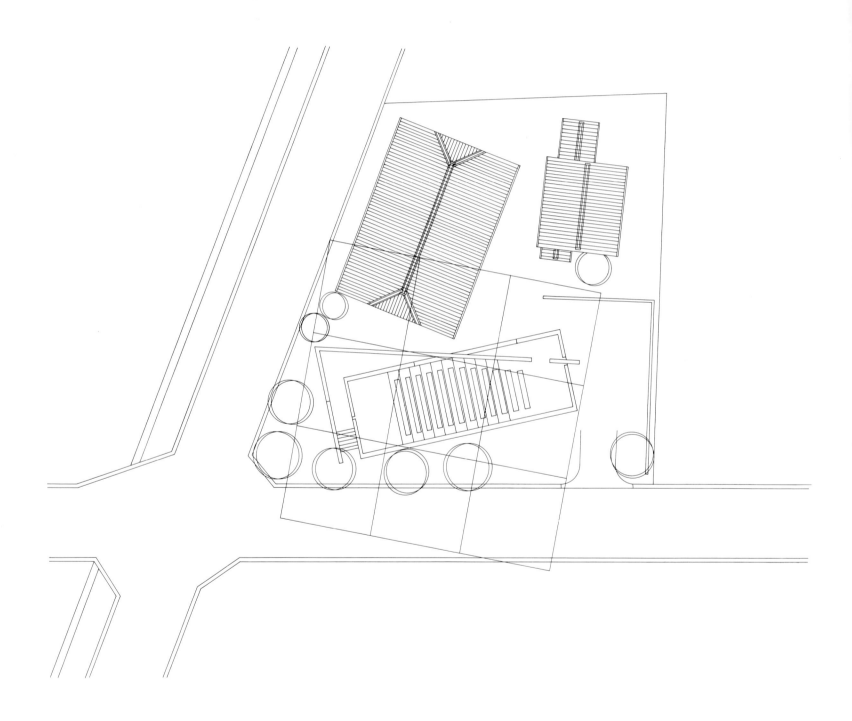

0   5m

0   15ft

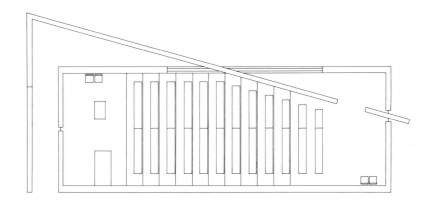

0 _____ 5m

0 _____ 15ft

Floor plan

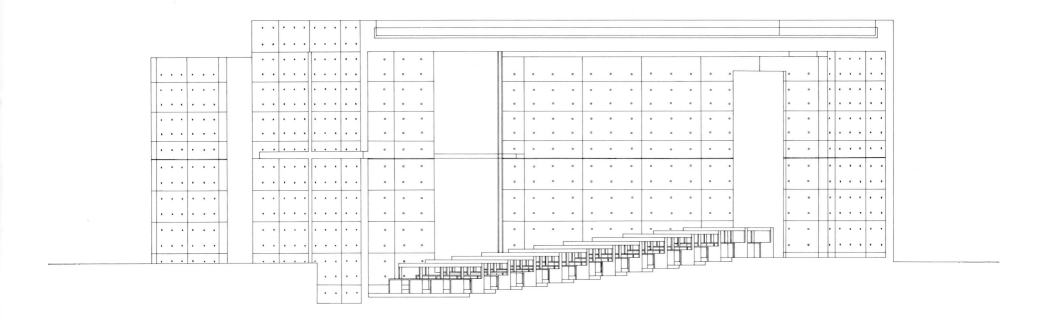

Section

0 _____ 2m

0 _____ 6ft

CEILING, WALL : EXPOSED CONCRETE

LIGHTING
FITTINGS

FIXED FLOAT GLASS t 6

FLOOR : BOARD t 36 OIL STAIN FINISH
(USED FOR TEMPORARY SCAFFOLD
ON CONSTRUCTION SITE)

18,000

2,850   200   2,850
5,900

200

7,000

3,950

1,600

t = 1,950

190   190
380

190   190
380

6,280

150

250

100

325   325
650

140 140
280

150

2,292

3,600

2,292

380
180   80
80   20   20

180
75   30   75

150

380
80   20   180   20   80
105   17   50   8

80

70   150

140   140
280

50

2,292

0   100mm

0   4in

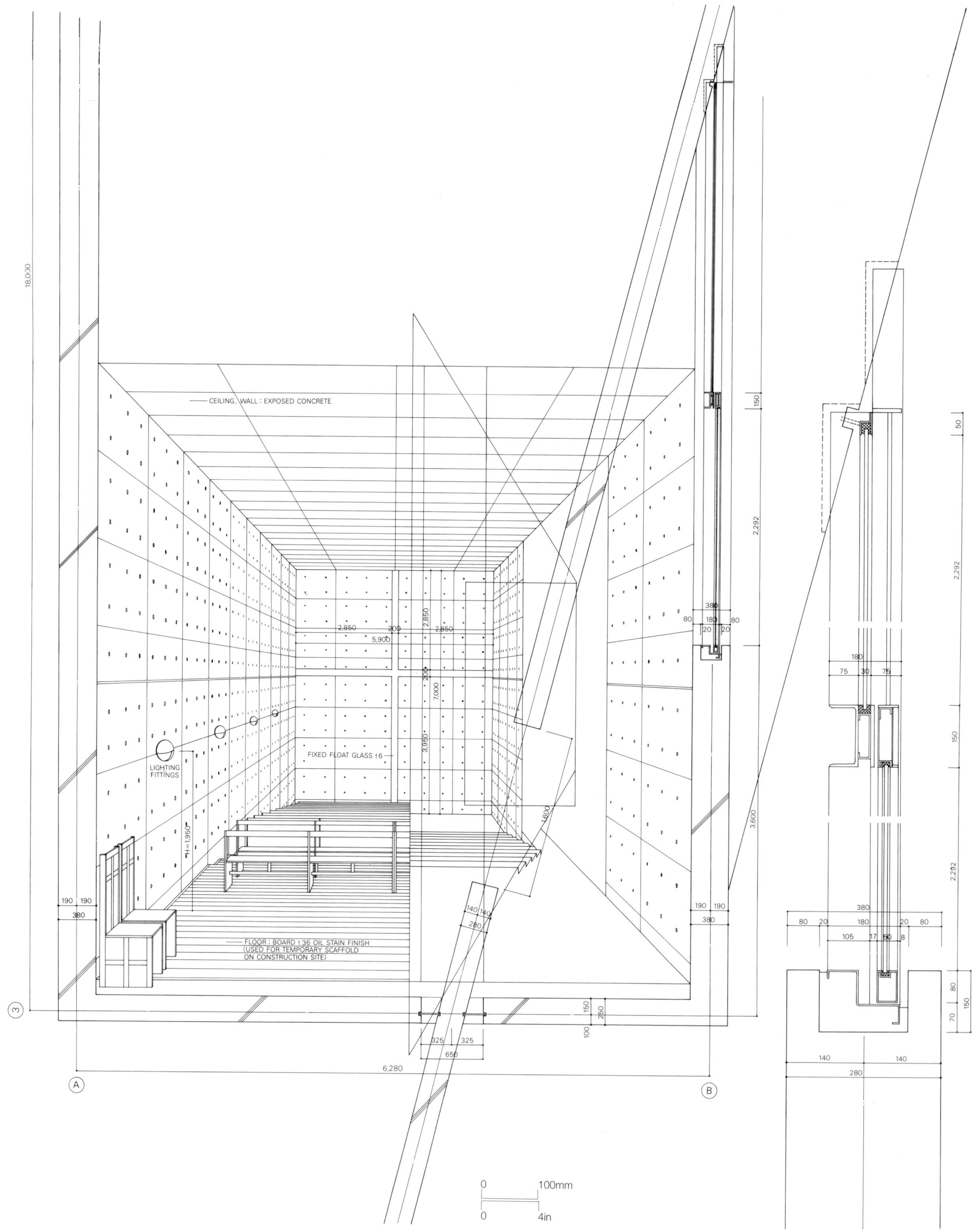

Perspective and details of furniture

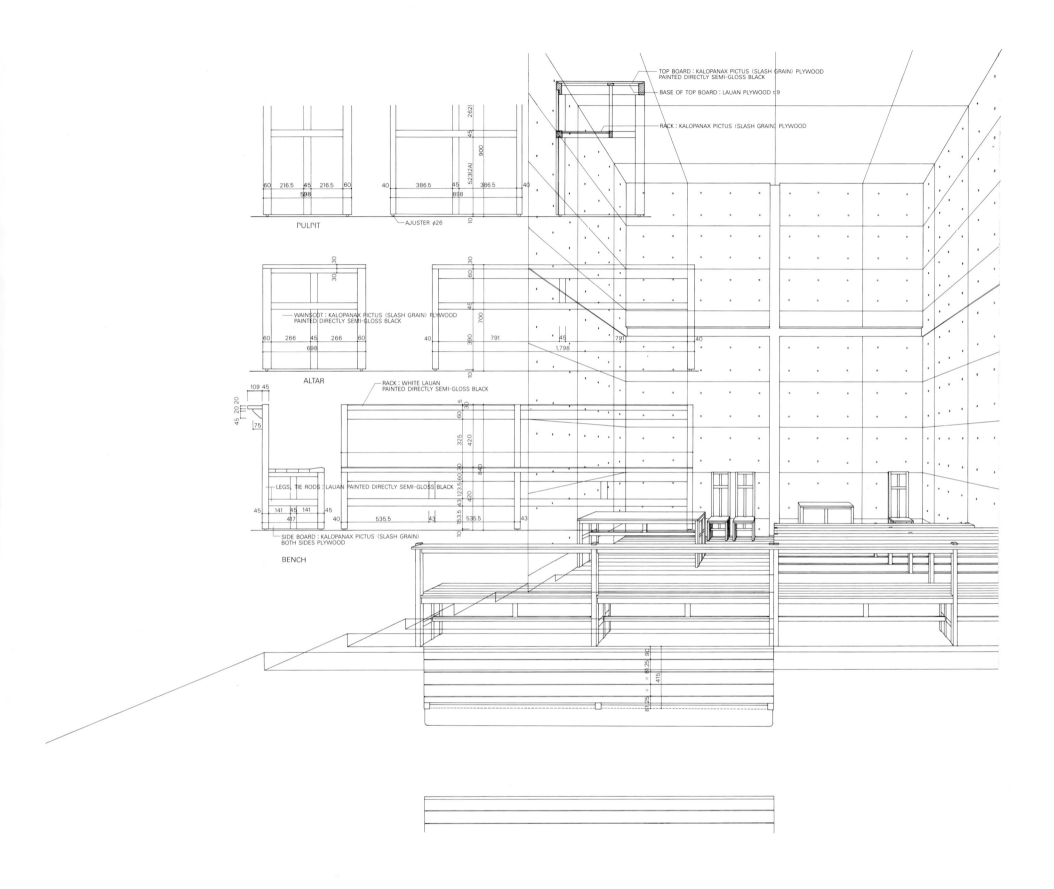

TOP BOARD : KALOPANAX PICTUS (SLASH GRAIN) PLYWOOD
PAINTED DIRECTLY SEMI-GLOSS BLACK

BASE OF TOP BOARD : LAUAN PLYWOOD t9

RACK : KALOPANAX PICTUS (SLASH GRAIN) PLYWOOD

PULPIT

AJUSTER φ26

WAINSCOT : KALOPANAX PICTUS (SLASH GRAIN) PLYWOOD
PAINTED DIRECTLY SEMI-GLOSS BLACK

ALTAR

RACK : WHITE LAUAN
PAINTED DIRECTLY SEMI-GLOSS BLACK

LEGS, TIE RODS : LAUAN PAINTED DIRECTLY SEMI-GLOSS BLACK

SIDE BOARD : KALOPANAX PICTUS (SLASH GRAIN)
BOTH SIDES PLYWOOD

BENCH

0   500mm

0   18in

Author's acknowledgements

I am indebted to Tadao Ando for his invaluable assistance, both in giving his time to explain each project, and in making it possible for me to visit the buildings. His office, in particular Hiromitsu Kuwata, helped with the drawings and supplied essential data, in addition to checking the draft of my essay.

Photographic credits

The publishers would like to thank the following for providing illustrations: Tadao Ando Architect & Associates: figs 1, 8, 9, 11–18; 20–32, 35, 38–41, 44, 45, 50, 54, 56, 59, 60, 63, 65–67, and pp 30, 31, 32 (top), 35, 37, 38–39, 41, 46–48, back cover; Shinkenchiku-sha: front cover, and figs 33, 34, 42, 43, 49, 53, 55, 61, 62, 64, 68, and pp 24–29, 32 (left), 33, 36, 40, 42–45; Yoshio Shiratori: p 34; The Bridgeman Art Library: fig 47; Martin Charles: fig 52; Philip Drew: figs 6, 7, 10, 19, 37, 51; Japan National Tourist Organization: figs 2, 3, 4, 5, 46; Staatliche Museen zu Berlin/Preußischer Kulturbesitz Nationalgalerie: fig 48.

Select bibliography

Books and periodicals: special issues
'Tadao Ando', *Japan Architect*, Tokyo, May 1982.
'Tadao Ando', *Japan Architect*, Tokyo, January 1991.
'Tadao Ando 1 1972–1987', *GA Architect*, No 8, Tokyo, 1987.
'Tadao Ando 2 1988–1993', *GA Architect*, No 12, Tokyo, 1993.
Tadao Ando Details, ADA Edita, Tokyo, 1991.
'Tadao Ando', *L'Architecture d'aujourd'hui*, No 255, February 1988.
Tadao Ando, Academy Editions Monograph No 14, London, 1990.
'Tadao Ando 1983–1990', *El Croquis*, No 44, Madrid, 1990.
'Tadao Ando 1989–1992', *El Croquis*, No 58, Madrid, 1993.
Tadao Ando: Beyond Horizons in Architecture, Tokyo, 1992.
Chaslin, François, *Tadao Ando – Minimalisme*, Paris, 1982.
Frampton, Kenneth (ed), *Tadao Ando: Buildings, Projects, Writings*, New York, 1984.
Frampton, Kenneth (ed), *Tadao Ando, The Yale Studio & Current Works*, New York, 1989.
Frampton, Kenneth (ed), *Tadao Ando, The Museum of Modern Art*, exhibition catalogue, New York, 1991.
Nitschke, Gunter, *From Shinto to Ando: Studies in Architectural Anthropology in Japan*, Academy Editions, London, 1993.

Tadao Ando: writings
'A wedge in circumstances', *Japan Architect*, 243, Vol 52, No 6, June 1977, pp 73–6.
'New relations between the space and the person', *Japan Architect*, No 247, October–November 1977, pp 43–6.
'Meet the architect: Tadao Ando', *GA Houses No 6*, Tokyo, October 1979, pp 172–205.
'From self-enclosed Modern architecture to Universality', *Japan Architect*, May 1982, p 6 ff.
'Representation and abstraction', *Japan Architect*, No 372, April 1988, p 8.
'Jun Port Island Building, 1985, and Kidosaki Residence, 1986', *Architectural Design*, Vol 58, No 5/6, 1988, pp 54–60.
'Abstraction serving reality', *Progressive Architecture*, Vol lxxi, No 2, February 1990, p 84.
'Collezione', *Japan Architect*, No 395, March 1990, pp 51–60.

Articles on the work of Tadao Ando
Akasaka, Yoshiaki, 'From confrontation to liberation: metamorphoses of spaces seen in the works of Tadao Ando', *Japan Architect*, No 342, October 1985, pp 27–9.
Bognar, Botond, 'Tadao Ando: a redefinition of Space, Time and Existence', *Architectural Design*, Vol 51, No 5, 1981, pp 25–6.
Bognar, Botond, 'Latest work of Tadao Ando', *Architectural Review*, Vol clxxii, No 1029, November 1982, pp 68–74.
'Chapel and Theatre on the Water', *Japan Architect*, No 272, April 1988, pp 43–51.
'Chapel on the Water' and 'Chapel of the Light', *Japan Architect*, No 386, June 1989, pp 6–17, 18–9.
'Church with the Light', *Japan Architect*, No 391–92, November–December 1989, pp 25–33.
Frampton, Kenneth, 'Synthesis of opposites', *L'Architecture d'aujourd'hui*, No 255, February 1988, pp 34–35.
Miyake, Kiichi, 'The path from Minimalism', *Japan Architect*, No 372, April 1988, pp 40–42.
Takeyama, Kiyoshi, 'Tadao Ando: heir to a tradition', *Perspecta*, No 20, Yale, 1983, pp 163–180.
'New version of the Old Row House', *Japan Architect*, No 243, Vol 52, No 6, June 1977, pp 57–64.
'Rose Garden', *Japan Architect*, 245, Vol 52, No 8, August 1977, pp 19–28.
Taki, Koji, 'The work of Fumihiko Maki and Tadao Ando', *Japan Architect*, No 319–320, November–December, 1983, pp 57–60.
Watanabe, Hiroshi, 'Tadao Ando: the architecture of denial,' *Japan Architect*, No 301, May 1982, pp 50–55.

Statistics

Church on the Water
Location: Tomamu, Yufutsu County, Hokkaido, Japan
Design: September 1985–April 1988
Construction: April 1988–September 1988
Structure: reinforced concrete, 1 storey, 1 basement
Site area: 6,730sq m
Building area: 344.9sq m
Total floor area: 520sq m
Structural engineer: Ascoral Engineering Associates
General contractor: Obayashi Corporation Co Ltd

Church of the Light
Location: Ibaraki, Osaka, Japan
Design: January 1987–May 1988
Construction: May 1988–April 1989
Structure: reinforced concrete, 1 storey
Site area: 836sq m
Building area: 113sq m
Total floor area: 113sq m
Structural engineer: Ascoral Engineering Associates
General contractor: Tatsumi Construction Co Ltd

Notes

1 Kenneth Frampton, *Modern Architecture: A Critical History*, London, 1980, p 297.
2 Kenneth Frampton, 'Towards a Critical Regionalism: six points for an architecture of resistance', in Hal Foster (ed), *The Anti Aesthetic: Essays on Postmodern Culture*, Washington DC, 1983, p 16.
3 *Modern Architecture: A Critical History*, *op cit*, p 297.
4 See Hiroshi Watanabe, 'Tadao Ando: the architecture of denial,' *Japan Architect*, No 301, May 1982, p 55.
5 Geometry provides the overall framework; this determines each aspect and the relationship to the landscape produced by its parts. Ando has stated: 'When, in this endeavour, the use of geometry centres on circles and squares – or their precise division, multiplication, diffusion, and transformation – the "architectural place" will respond, in reverberation, in this instance, regardless of this non-arbitrary character, condenses all varieties of meaning – or conversely, scatters it outward – transforming it endlessly.' from Tadao Ando, 'In dialogue with geometry: the creation of "landscape"', in 'Tadao Ando 1988–1993', *GA Architect*, No 12, Tokyo, 1993, p 25.
6 See Point 3: the free designing of the ground plan, Pierre Jeanneret: 'Five points towards a new architecture', 1926, in Ulrich Conrads, *Programmes and Manifestoes on 20th-Century Architecture*, London, 1970, pp 99–100.
7 *The Iliad of Homer*, translated by A Land, W Leaf and E Myers, Bk VII, pp 128, 211, 212.
8 J.B. Bury, *A History of Greece*, third edition, London, 1972, pp 472–4.
9 William Willets, *Chinese Art*, Vol 2, Harmondsworth, 1958, p 662.
10 From Kenneth Frampton, 'Synthesis of opposites', in *L'Architecture d'aujourd'hui*, February 1988, p 34.
11 Tadao Ando, 'Church on the Water', in *Japan Architect* Special issue, January 1991, p 110.
12 The Abbey at Sénanque, Provence, France, gave Ando an appreciation of the compelling power that springs from buildings when the architect contrives a unique logic for the architecture which is aligned with the logic latent in the surrounding land. Tadao Ando, 'In dialogue with geometry: the creation of "landscape"', *op cit*, p 24.

3 ARCHITECTURE's

PLACES OF WORSHIP

Sir Christopher Wren
St Paul's Cathedral

Jože Plečnik
Church of the Sacred Heart

Tadao Ando
Church on the Water
Church of the Light

James S. Russell, AIA, is editor-at-large at *Architectural Record* magazine. He also writes for publications including *The New York Times*, the *Philadelphia Enquirer* and *Harvard Design Magazine*. He teaches at Columbia University, New York, and is the principal of a consulting firm, WorkDesign.

Vaughan Hart is Reader in Architectural History at the University of Bath Department of Architecture. He has also taught at the Architectural Association and Cambridge University. He is an expert on the Baroque period and is translating Serlio's *Architettura*.

Ivan Margolius is a practising architect of Czech origin working in London. He is also author of *Cubism in Architecture and the Applied Arts*, *Skoda Laurin & Klement, Tatra: The Legacy of Hans Ledwinka* and *Prague: A Guide to Twentieth-Century Architecture*.

Philip Drew is an architectural historian and critic based in Australia. He has written numerous studies of leading twentieth-century contemporary architects and has written widely on Japanese contemporary architecture. He is the Australian correspondent for the international Tokyo magazine *A+U*.

Phaidon Press Limited
Regent's Wharf
All Saints Street
London N1 9PA

Places of Worship first published 1999
© 1999 Phaidon Press Limited
ISBN 0 7148 3877 2

A CIP catalogue record for this book is available
from the British Library.

Printed in Hong Kong

St Paul's Cathedral originally published in
Architecture in Detail series 1995
© 1995 Phaidon Press Limited
Church of the Sacred Heart originally published in
Architecture in Detail series 1995
© 1995 Phaidon Press Limited
Church on the Water, Church of the Light
originally published in Architecture in Detail
series 1996
© 1996 Phaidon Press Limited